Reproducible Activities

Using the Standards

Building Grammar & Writing Skills

Grade 2

By
Q. L. Pearce

Instructional Fair
An imprint of Carson-Dellosa Publishing LLC
Greensboro, North Carolina

Instructional Fair

Author: Q. L. Pearce
Editors: Jeanine Manfro, Christine Hood

Instructional Fair
An imprint of Carson-Dellosa Publishing LLC
PO Box 35665
Greensboro, NC 27425 USA

ISBN 978-0-74241-802-8
102107800

Introduction

Communication skills, both written and verbal, are critical in today's society. Before entering the school system, children have a general concept of structure and grammar; however, continued success in school is dependent on children's general knowledge of basic grammar and writing skills. In this book, we will build on that foundation through the use of activities designed specifically to reflect NCTE English Language Standards at the first-grade level.

With standards teaching and testing at an all-time high, it is important that children not only understand the basics of grammar and writing, but also how to demonstrate their knowledge through testing and assessment. This book includes over 100 activities that provide further progress with basic skills in grammar and writing essential for future academic success. From alphabet review to creative writing and poetry, individual activities enhance curriculum, while offering flexibility and practice in each area.

For your convenience, you will find an overview of the 12 NCTE English Language Arts Standards (page 4), as well as an expanded Table of Contents (pages 5–8), which is organized into three easy-to-read columns. The first column lists the title of each activity and the skill (or skills) it teaches. The second column lists the number of the NCTE standard addressed by the activity, based on the Standards Grid. Any one activity may address one or several standards. Page numbers where you can find the activities are listed in the third column.

This book is divided into seven sections, according to skills: Basic Grammar Skills, Capitalization, Punctuation, Parts of Speech, Usage, Writing Strategies, and Writing Applications. Some activities are simple, while others are more challenging. All activities, however, are designed to guide the grade one student to a basic understanding of the English language and the writing process. A comprehensive Answer Key is located at the back of the book, beginning on page 125.

Published by Instructional Fair. Copyright protected.

English Language Arts Standards

1. Read a wide range of texts.

2. Read a wide range of literature.

3. Apply a variety of strategies to comprehend and interpret texts.

4. Use spoken, written, and visual language to communicate effectively.

5. Use a variety of strategies while writing and use elements of the writing
process to communicate.

6. Apply knowledge of language structure and conventions, media techniques,
figurative language, and genre to create, critique, and discuss texts.

7. Research issues and interests, pose questions, and gather data to
communicate discoveries.

8. Work with a variety of technological and other resources to collect
information   and to communicate knowledge.

9. Understand and respect the differences in language use across cultures, regions,
and social roles.

10. Students whose first language is not English use their first language
to develop
competencies in English and other content areas.

11. Participate in a variety of literary communities.

12. Use spoken, written, and visual language to accomplish purposes.

Published by Instructional Fair. Copyright protected.   0-7424-1802-2 *Building Grammar & Writing Skills*

Table of Contents	Standards Reflected	Page
Introduction		3
Part I: Grammar		
Basic Grammar Skills		
Bountiful Blends	4, 6	9
Treasure Teams	4, 6	10
Vowel Venture	4, 6	11
Short Vowels	4, 6	12
Zoo Clues	3, 4, 6	13
Sneaky, Silent E	4, 6	14
Capitalization		
Letter Practice	4	15
Starting Sentences	4, 6	16
Capital "I"	3, 4, 6	17
Names and Places	4, 6	18
Tricky Titles	4, 6	19
Books and Magazines	4, 6	20
Calendar Capitals	4, 6	21
Ready for Review	4, 6	22
Punctuation		
At the End	3, 4, 6	23
Long to Short	4, 6	24
What's the Question?	3, 4, 5, 6, 12	25
Exciting Exclamations	3, 4, 6, 7	26
Sentence Endings	3, 4, 5, 6, 12	27
Pause for Commas	4, 6	28
Make a List	4, 5, 6, 12	29
Whose Is It?	3, 4, 6	30
Quote Me	3, 4, 6	31
Ready for Review	3, 4, 6	32
Parts of Speech		
Pretty Presents	4, 6	33
Person, Place, or Thing?	4, 6	34
Practice with Nouns	4, 6	35
Common or Proper?	4, 6	36
Proper Places	4, 6	37
Days and Dates	4, 6	38
Towers of Nouns	4, 5, 6, 12	39
How Many?	4, 6	40
More Than One	4, 6	41

0-7424-1802-2 *Building Grammar & Writing Skills*

Table of Contents

Published by Instructional Fair. Copyright protected.   0-7424-1802-2 *Building Grammar & Writing Skills*

Table of Contents	Standards Reflected	Page

Part III: Writing Applications

Published by Instructional Fair. Copyright protected. 0-7424-1802-2 *Building Grammar & Writing Skills*

Name _____ Date _____

Bountiful Blends

Some letters work together as a "team." Together, these letters make one sound, called a **blend.**

Look at the blends below. Then choose a blend to fill in each blank and complete the sentences.

bl   cr   sk   sn   tr   st   sw   fl   pl

1. I have a _____ ue _____ ayon.

2. There is an old _____ ing in the _____ ee.

3. John likes to _____ ay in the _____ ow.

4. Lisa watched the _____ ail _____ awl slowly past.

5. The _____ unk smelled the _____ ower.

0-7424-1802-2 *Building Grammar & Writing Skills*

Name _____ Date _____

Treasure Teams

These letter pairs work together to make brand-new sounds:

sh th ph ch

bath
chick
chair

tooth
shoe
photo

chime
fish
phone

ship
graph
thumb

Look at each letter pair in on the left side of the page. Find three words by the treasure box that include the letter pair. Write them on the lines.

1. sh _____

_____

_____

2. ch _____

_____

_____

3. th _____

_____

_____

4. ph _____

_____

_____

Choose one word from each group. Write a sentence using the word.

1. _____

2. _____

3. _____

10

Name _____ Date _____

Vowel Venture

The letters **a, e, i, o,** and **u** are vowels. They can make different sounds.

The name of each object below begins with a vowel. Fill in the vowel and color the picture.

1. _____ pe

2. _____ lephant

3. _____ nsect

4. _____ wl

5. _____ mbrella

Think of other words that begin with vowels. Write a word on each line that begins with the vowel shown.

1. a _____

2. e _____

3. i _____

4. o _____

5. u _____

Name _____ Date _____

Short Vowels

Some vowels have a short sound, like **a** in **cat** or **u** in **up.**

Read the names of things you might see at the beach. Write the words with short vowel sounds on the lines below.

1._____ 2. _____ 3. _____ 4. _____

5._____ 6. _____ 7. _____ 8. _____

Name _____ Date_____

Zoo Clues

Long vowels say their own name, like **a** in **ape** or **e** in **eel.**

Read the zoo clues. Then choose the correct long vowel words from the Word Box to complete the puzzle.

ACROSS

2. I roar!

4. I have stripes.

6. I am a jungle cat.

DOWN

1. I slither.

3. I can have antlers.

5. I can also be called a gorilla.

7. I am a good climber.

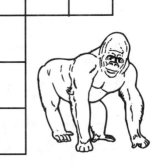

Word Box				
lion	giraffe	ape	alligator	tiger
hawk	deer	snake	moose	lizard
bat	zebra	monkey	goat	wolf

Name _____ Date _____

Sneaky, Silent E

The letter **e** at the end of a word can change a short vowel to a long vowel. The **e** is silent.

Example: bit + e = bite

Read each sentence. Underline the word that is incorrect. Then rewrite the sentence, adding a silent **e** to the word you underlined.

1. Staci at the crunchy apple.

_____

2. The clown gave Tom a candy can.

_____

3. I want to fly my kit.

_____

4. Jared took car of his puppy.

_____

5. Rip peaches are good to eat.

_____

6. Mom wrote a not to my teacher.

_____

7. The pin tree is green.

_____

8. Sara's new kitten is so cut!

_____

0-7424-1802-2 *Building Grammar & Writing Skills*

Name _____ Date _____

Letter Practice

Look at the books on the shelves. Color the books with capital letters **red.** Color the other letters **blue.**

0-7424-1802-2 *Building Grammar & Writing Skills*

Name _____ Date _____

Starting Sentences

The first word in a sentence begins with a capital letter.

Read the sentences. Rewrite the first word in each sentence with a capital letter.

1. (birds) _____ fly south in the winter.

2. (my) _____ grandfather is funny.

3. (yesterday) _____ it rained.

4. (the) _____ girl ate a sandwich.

5. (river) _____ rafting is fun for the whole family.

6. (andy's) _____ dog won a blue ribbon.

7. (summer) _____ is my favorite season.

8. (high) _____ wind blew down the sign.

9. (do) _____ you like popcorn?

10. (run) _____ really fast!

0-7424-1802-2 *Building Grammar & Writing Skills*

Name _____ Date _____

Capital "I"

The word **I** is always capitalized. Write the missing **I**'s in the paragraph. Some of them should be capitalized, and some should not.

Kaitlyn wanted to make pancakes for breakfast w_____th her dad. They took out the _____ngredients. They were out of m_____lk.

"_____will drive to the store," her dad said. Wh_____le he was gone, Ka_____tly measured the other_____ngred_____ents.

_____am back," her dad sa_____d.

_____"I am glad you are," Ka_____tlyn repl_____ed. "_____am getting very hungry. May_____pour the m_____lk?" Dad handed her the m_____lk. She m_____xed the batter and poured_____t on the gr_____ddle. Dad fl_____pped the pancakes as they cooked. They ate the pancakes w_____th maple syrup.

"These are the best pancakes_____have ever tasted," Dad sa_____d.

"_____th_____nk you are r_____ght," Ka_____tlyn agreed with a sm_____le.

0-7424-1802-2 *Building Grammar & Writing Skills*

Name _____ Date _____

Names and Places

The names of specific people, pets, and places begin with a capital letter.
Read the postcards. Circle the letters that should be capitals.

1.

Dear paul,
     We are having lots
of fun in montana. We
went fishing at the choro
river. We saw the
sawtooth mountains.
Tonight we are going to
stay in helena. That is
the state capital.
     Your friend,
     angela

paul davis
555 porter street
davis, delaware
12345

2.

Dear mom and dad,
     I love camp azalea!
We went for a hike in red
rock valley. Tomorrow I
want to visit the dean
thomas library. It has lots
of books about dogs. I
miss buddy. Give him a
pat on the head for me.
     Love,
     dylan

mr. and mrs. worski
123 covington court
mayfield, texas
54321

18

Name _____ Date _____

Tricky Titles

Sometimes people have titles before their names, like **Mr., Mrs., Ms., Miss, Doctor,** and **Professor.** Titles begin with a capital letter. Words like **aunt, uncle,** and **cousin** are only capitalized when they come before the person's name, like **Aunt Martha.**

Taylor made nametags for a family reunion. He forgot to capitalize the names. Rewrite each name with the correct capital letters.

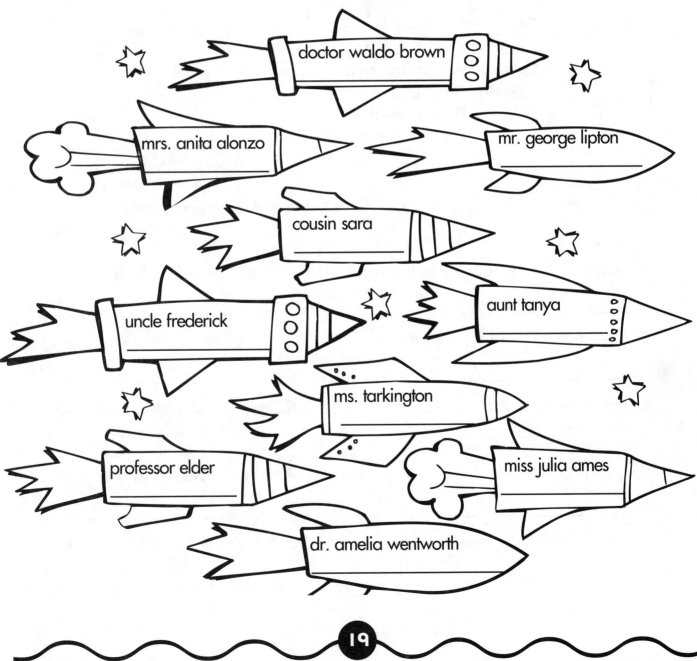

doctor waldo brown

mrs. anita alonzo

mr. george lipton

cousin sara

aunt tanya

uncle frederick

ms. tarkington

professor elder

miss julia ames

dr. amelia wentworth

19

0-7424-1802-2 *Building Grammar & Writing Skills*

Name _____ Date _____

Books and Magazines

Capitalize titles of books, magazines, poems, songs, and movies.

Hint: Unless they are the first word in a title, you don't have to capitalize these little words: at, by, for, in, of, to, with, and, but, or, a, an, the.

Examples: **O**ld **Y**eller (book)
   The **W**heels on the **B**us (song)
   Sports **I**llustrated for **K**ids (magazine)
   Little **B**oy **B**lue (poem)
   Cats and **D**ogs (movie)

Read the titles below. Rewrite each title with the correct capital letters.

1. how much is that doggie in the window?

_____

2. the biography of helen keller

_____

3. horse lover magazine

_____

4. green eggs and ham

_____

5. twinkle, twinkle little star

_____

6. the big book of lizards

_____

7. mary had a little lamb

_____

8. how to train your cat with treats

_____

9. school days magazine

_____

10. america the beautiful

_____

20

Name _____ Date _____

Calendar Capitals

Capitalize the names of days, months, and holidays.
Rewrite each sentence with the correct capital letters.

1. allen goes to soccer practice on tuesdays and thursdays.

   _____

2. we celebrate the fourth of july by boating on the lake.

   _____

3. jenn's dance recital is on valentine's day.

   _____

4. kelly went to ellen's house on friday.

   _____

5. my sister will be six years old in may.

   _____

6. In january, we always go sledding on saturday mornings.

   _____

7. jamie's favorite holiday is hanukah, which comes in december.

   _____

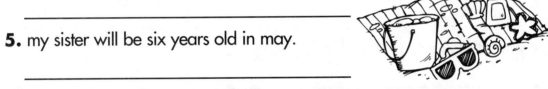

Finish these sentences. Capitalize the days, months, and holidays.

8. I was born in the month of _____.

9. My favorite holiday is _____.

10. _____ is my favorite day of the week.

0-7424-1802-2 *Building Grammar & Writing Skills*

Name _____ Date _____

Ready for Review

Rewrite each sentence with the correct capital letters.

1. my friends and i go to bear creek school.

_____

2. byron has a dog named tilly and a cat named weed.

_____

3. my teacher is mrs. jamison.

_____

4. jerry went to wyoming last year for Father's Day.

_____

5. alicia read the wind in the willows.

_____

6. aunt cindy is my favorite aunt.

_____

7. brandon celebrates christmas with his grandparents.

_____

8. tina wrote a poem called jumpy bumpy jack.

_____

9. dr. lopez made a special visit to see rex last saturday.

_____

10. mother's day is in the month of may.

_____

0-7424-1802-2 *Building Grammar & Writing Skills*

Name _____ Date _____

At the End

A **period (.)** is used at the end of a sentence that tells something or gives a command.

Examples:

Telling Sentence: I am going to eat dinner.
Command: Eat your dinner.

Read the sentences. Put a period at the end of each sentence that tells something or gives a command.

1. Hawaii is the fiftieth state

2. Sit down

3. Do you like peppermint

4. William read his book quietly

5. Where is your homework

6. Do your homework neatly

7. My dog has floppy ears

8. Read your book

9. My dad snores

10. What is your favorite food

0-7424-1802-2 *Building Grammar & Writing Skills*

Name _____ Date _____

Long to Short

Some long words can be written as abbreviations. An **abbreviation** is a shorter way to write a word. It has a period at the end.

Read the list of words. Draw a line from each abbreviation to the word it stands for.

Dr.	January
Sept.	Mister
Jan.	September
Mr.	December
Sun.	February
Dec.	August
St.	Wednesday
Tues.	Doctor
Feb.	Sunday
Oct.	Thursday
Wed.	Avenue
Thurs.	Friday
Aug.	October
Fri.	Tuesday
Ave.	Street

24

   0-7424-1802-2 *Building Grammar & Writing Skills*

Name _____ Date _____

What's the Question?

Asking sentences end with a question mark. **(?)**

Read the sentences. Put a question mark after each question.

1. Look at this book

2. Did you eat lunch yet

3. I'm cold

4. Are you cold

5. How old is Jonathan's sister

6. Where does Natalie live

7. Wendy ran home

8. Why did Frank write in his book

9. Don't touch that

10. Where is my pen

Sentences that begin with the asking words **who, what, when, where, why,** and **how** usually ends with a question mark. Make up your own asking questions. Remember to end each with a question mark.

Who

What

When

Where

Why

How

25

Name _____ Date _____

Exciting Exclamations

Use an exclamation point (**!**) to show surprise or strong feelings.

Put the correct ending mark at the end of each sentence. (**. ? !**) Then write the sentence below the "matching" picture.

1. I can't believe we won
2. I don't like this book
3. That is nice
4. Do you want to keep it
5. Wow, it's just what I wanted

6. It's so cold
7. I don't like that book
8. Watch out
9. Is that your glass
10. May I help you

11. _____

12. _____

13. _____

14. _____

0-7424-1802-2 *Building Grammar & Writing Skills*

Name _____ Date _____

Sentence Endings

Read the sentences about the pet store. Put the correct ending mark at the end of each sentence. **(. ? !)**

1. That bunny is so cute

2. Do you have a pet

3. My cat loves tuna fish

4. I think turtles are fun

5. Look at that

6. Have you ever seen a ferret

7. How much does that birdcage cost

8. My dog likes to ride in the car

9. Wow, his teeth are sharp

10. I know the owner of this pet store

Write three sentences about the pet store—a telling sentence, an asking sentence, and an exclamation.

11. _____

12. _____

13. _____

27

Name _____ Date _____

Pause for Commas

A **comma** separates words. It tells the reader to pause. Use a comma between the day and year in a date. Use a comma between the city and state in an address.

Examples: August 9, 2002

Austin, Texas

Read these invitations and envelopes. Put commas in the correct places.

It's a birthday party!
Cassie Wyman

Date: October 9 2002
423 Center Street

Place: Pizza Paradise
Littleton Maine 89764

Cassie Wyman

423 Center Street

Littleton Maine 89764

You're invited to a sleepover!
Lin Nance

Date: January 23 2003
37 West Road

Place: My house
Tampa Florida 62341

Lin Nance

37 West Road

Tampa Florida 62341

Boo! It's a Halloween party!
Tyrone Hilliard

Date: October 31 2003
10024 Wells Avenue

Place: My house
Claremont California 91734

Tyrone Hilliard

10024 Wells Avenue

Claremont California
91734

Splish, splash!
Come to my pool party!
Armando Santos

Date: June 16 2003
562 Justice Street, #38

Place: Manfield Park
West Orange NJ 07052

Armando Santos

562 Justice Street, #38

West Orange NJ 07052

28

Name _____ Date _____

Make a List

When you write a list of words, put a comma between each item in the list.

Example: I like apples, bananas, oranges, and cherries.
Read the sentences and add commas where they
are needed.

1. My mother grows roses daisies and violets in her garden.

2. My brother's name is John Henry Mills.

3. There are maple pine oak and elm trees on my street.

4. In my class we study spelling math history and art.

5. Claire Phil Tammy Joe and I went to the movies together.

6. Tana brought her dogs Peaches Romeo and Clyde to the park.

7. Mina's favorite colors are yellow purple blue and pink.

Complete each sentences with a list. Put at least three items in each list. Remember to use commas.

8. My favorite foods are _____

9. I like the sports _____

10. When I go on vacation, I take _____

29

Name _____ Date _____

Whose Is It?

An apostrophe shows ownership. Add an apostrophe and **s** to show who or what something belongs to.

Examples: Riley's computer; the girl's crayons
Read the story. Put apostrophes where they belong.

Cameron and Marie were playing in the park near a tree. The trees leaves were thick and green. Cameron saw a birds nest in the tree. Marie saw a squirrel in the tree. The squirrels fur was soft and gray. A small dog ran across the grass toward them. The dogs leash dragged on the ground. The dogs owner ran behind. "Sorry!" he called when he caught the leash. "I guess everyone loves the park," Marie laughed.

0-7424-1802-2 *Building Grammar & Writing Skills*

Name _____ Date _____

Quote Me

Use quotation marks (" ") around the exact words someone says.

Example: "I love you," Carrie told her dad.
Read each group of sentences. Underline the sentence
that includes a quote. Add quotation marks around
what the person said.

1. Jill won a medal at the swim meet.

Jill won a medal, yelled the coach.

Jill's medals were won at the swim meet.

2. The dog barked at Todd.

The trainer talked to the dog's owner.

Todd said, I like dogs.

3. I'm going to walk to school, said Sue.

Sue said I could ride her bike.

Sue told me to be careful.

4. Bryan yelled at his little brother.

Hit the ball! Bryan yelled at his little brother.

Bryan hit the ball harder than Michael.

5. Emma said that she likes apple pie.

Apple pie is Emma's favorite dessert.

I love apple pie, Emma told me.

0-7424-1802-2 *Building Grammar & Writing Skills*

Name _____ Date _____

Ready for Review

There are **15 mistakes** in this paragraph. Circle them
Then correct them.

Mando put paper a pencil an eraser and markers on
his desk he was going to start his report on
President Abraham lincoln? He wrote the date
February 16 1809. That is when Lincoln was
born, he said aloud to his cat, Simba "would
you like to know more about him. You'll
just have to wait until I finish my report."
Mando reached down to scratch simba on
the neck, and the cat purred and purred.
Okay, back to work," mando said.

0-7424-1802-2 *Building Grammar & Writing Skills*

Name _____ Date _____

Pretty Presents

A **noun** names a person, place, or thing.

Examples: mother; beach; ribbon

Read the words on each gift. Color gifts with nouns on them.

 trees, tiger, jungle

 sleep, laugh, pretty

 mouse, cheese, tail

 king, crown, castle

 pull, climb, blue

 boat, ocean, wave

 chair, bed, couch

 pink, tiny, say

 green, huge, fun

 ball, toy, doll

0-7424-1802-2 *Building Grammar & Writing Skills*

Name _____ Date _____

Person, Place, or Thing?

A **noun** names a person, place, or thing. Circle the nouns in each sentence.

1. A frog lives in the pond.

2. My teacher drives a truck.

3. The girl ate a hot dog.

4. My doctor walked me to my car.

5. The street is lined with trees.

6. That box is full of trash.

7. The ocean is full of colorful fish.

8. The player threw the football down the field.

Write each noun you circled in the correct column.

PERSON	**PLACE**	**THING**

0-7424-1802-2 *Building Grammar & Writing Skills*

Name _____ Date _____

Practice with Nouns

A **noun** names a person, place, or thing. Underline the nouns in each sentence.

1. The boy plays soccer. (2 nouns)
2. I planted a vegetable garden. (2 nouns)
3. My sister planted a tree at school. (3 nouns)
4. These gloves are red and white. (1 noun)
5. My grandma gave us cookies and milk after lunch. (4 nouns)
6. His aunt visited the museum last fall. (2 nouns)
7. Please wear a sweater. (1 noun)
8. Sometimes I read a book in bed. (2 nouns)
9. She bought milk, eggs, bread, and fruit at the store. (5 nouns)
10. That dog chased my kite all over the park. (3 nouns)

Write the correct noun under each picture

11. _____ 12. _____ 13. _____

14. _____ 15. _____ 16. _____

0-7424-1802-2 *Building Grammar & Writing Skills*

Name _____ Date _____

Common or Proper?

A **common noun** names a general person, place, or thing. A **proper noun** names a specific person, place, or thing. Proper nouns begin with a capital letter.

Examples: **Common Nouns**   **Proper Nouns**

        dog   Bingo

        city   Tulsa

        girl   Mia

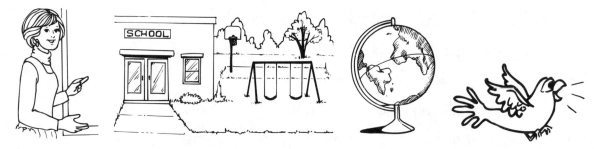

Write **C** next to the common nouns and **P** next to the proper nouns.

1. April _____   **2.** dog _____   **3.** Wednesday _____

4. Fifi _____   **5.** Pacific _____   **6.** lake _____

7. boy _____   **8.** Italy _____   **9.** Randi _____

10. flower _____   **11.** country _____   **12.** Smokey _____

13. New York _____   **14.** May _____   **15.** state _____

0-7424-1802-2 *Building Grammar & Writing Skills*

Name _____ Date _____

Proper Places

A **proper noun** names a specific person, place, or thing.

Read the sentences. Underline the proper nouns that should begin with a capital letter. Write them correctly on the lines.

1. I was born in new york city. _____

2. We live in orange county. _____

3. lake superior is the largest lake in the united states.

_____

_____

4. chloe spent her summer at camp willow.

_____

_____

5. When ted went to chicago he visited the sears tower.

_____

_____

6. bermuda is in the atlantic ocean.

_____

_____

7. The capital of michigan is lansing.

_____

_____

8. We had a picnic at lewis park. _____

9. Logan goes to ellis elementary school. _____

10. chelsea went swimming in the colorado river.

_____

_____

0-7424-1802-2 *Building Grammar & Writing Skills*

Name _____ Date _____

Days and Dates

Names of months, days of the week, and holidays are proper nouns.

Write the words from the Word Box in the correct columns. Make sure to begin each word with a capital letter.

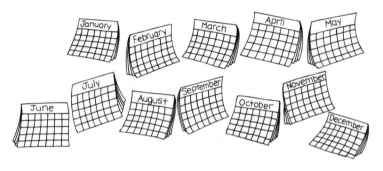

Word Box			
halloween	monday	friday	june
wednesday	april	mother's day	january
december	president's day	sunday	labor day
tuesday	february	valentine's day	thursday

DAYS	MONTHS	HOLIDAYS

38

Name _____ Date _____

Towers of Nouns

Read the list in each tower. Circle the proper nouns in each list.

1.	2.	3.	4.
goal	soccer ball	Coach Gorman	score
dog	rat	lizard	Buddy
Laurie	Brad	story	Oregon
Park Ave.	3rd Street	Disneyland	Times Square
Ford	key	car	tire
teacher	Mrs. Poole	school	notebook
river	lake	Indian Ocean	pond
day	Monday	Tuesday	holiday
Ohio	state	country	Crater Lake
girl	Yolanda	Fluffy	boy

Choose a proper noun from each list. Then write a sentence using the word or words.

5. _____

6. _____

7. _____

8. _____

0-7424-1802-2 *Building Grammar & Writing Skills*

Name _____ Date _____

How Many?

A plural noun tells about more than one person, place, or thing. To make most nouns plural, add an **s** at the end.

Examples: shoe shoes; pen pens; boy boys
Look at each picture. Write the number of objects. Then rewrite the word to make it plural.

Example:  balloon   <u>two balloons</u>

1. flower _____

2. clock _____

3. bat _____

4. pencil _____

5. book _____

6. snake _____

7. hat _____

8. ball _____

9. bird _____

10. apple _____

40

Name _____ Date _____

More Than One

If a noun ends in **s, ss, sh, ch,** or **x,** add **es** to make it plural.

Examples: gas   gases
                glass   glasses
                wish   wishes
                patch   patches
                mix   mixes

Underline the letter or letters at the end of each word that tell you how to make the plural. Write the plural nouns on the lines. The first one is done for you.

1.  kiss   <u>kisses</u>

2. watch _____

3. bus _____

4. fox _____

5. wash _____

6. grass _____

7. bush _____

8. box _____

0-7424-1802-2 *Building Grammar & Writing Skills*

Name _____ Date _____

Plenty of Plurals

Read the sentences. The words in parentheses should be plural. Write the new words on the lines.

1. My sister has many (doll). _____

2. Karen put her clothes in (box). _____

3. Kayla bought six new (dress). _____

4. I love to watch the (wave) on the ocean. _____

5. Anita cleaned the (brush) after painting the picture. _____

6. The boy made three (wish). _____

7. Our school (bus) are bright yellow. _____

8. Our city has five nice (park). _____

9. Bob washed the (dish) after dinner. _____

10. My (shoe) are worn out. _____

0-7424-1802-2 *Building Grammar & Writing Skills*

Name _____ Date _____

Special Plurals

Words that end in **y** are special. When a word ends in vowel-**y**, add **s** to make it plural.

Example: da**y** — day**s**
When a word ends in consonant-**y**, change the **y** to **i** and add **es**.

Example: ci**ty**—cit**ies**

Look at the pictures. Circle the correct plural below each picture.

1.

monkeys   monkies

2.

partys   parties

3.

babys   babies

4.

turkeys turkies

5.

valleys vallies

6.

storys stories

7.

flys flies

8.

cries cry

0-7424-1802-2 *Building Grammar & Writing Skills*

Name _____ Date _____

Ready for Review

Complete the puzzle by writing the correct plural form of each noun.

ACROSS

1. class
2. trip
4. speech
7. fax

DOWN

1. city
3. family
5. cat
6. turkey
8. tag

Name _____ Date _____

Verbs in Action

Verbs are action words. They tell what is happening in a sentence.

Example: Tyrese **runs** the race today.

Underline the verb in each sentence.

1. I hop over the fence.

2. Jack climbs the ladder.

3. Do not play in the hallway.

4. Jamie can run very fast.

5. Natalie works on her painting.

6. Terrell loves potato chips.

7. We shop on Sundays.

8. Lindsey draws very well.

Find and circle each verb from above in the puzzle. Words can go across or down.

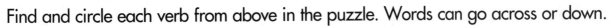

C	T	L	O	R	U	N	J	N	S
L	O	V	E	S	D	C	E	H	H
I	S	T	P	V	R	N	R	E	O
M	J	P	L	L	A	H	H	I	P
B	Q	N	A	V	W	O	R	K	S
S	W	G	Y	Y	S	P	R	O	W

45

0-7424-1802-2 *Building Grammar & Writing Skills*

Name _____ Date _____

More Verbs

Some **verbs** don't seem to show a lot of action. They tell about things we think, feel, and do.

Choose words from the clouds to complete each sentence.

learn   think   believe   hear   want

plan   know   dream   live   listen

1. Sometimes I _____ while I am asleep.

2. I do not _____ in space aliens.

3. I _____ in a house near my school.

4. The teacher asked us to _____ to the music.

5. Did you _____ that loud noise?

6. What do you _____ about this book?

7. I would like to _____ to play the piano.

8. I _____ how to say the Pledge of Allegiance.

9. Will you help me _____ my birthday party?

10. I _____ to go to the movies today.

46

0-7424-1802-2 *Building Grammar & Writing Skills*

Name _____ Date _____

Now and Then

Some **verbs** tell about actions happening now. Some tell about actions that happened in the past (these are called **past-tense** verbs).

Add **ed** to most verbs to show past tense. If the word already ends in **e,** just add **d.**

Examples: talk = action now   share = action now
                   talk**ed** = past action   share**d** = past action

Write each verb from the list in past tense. The first one is done for you.

PRESENT	PAST
help	helped
wash	_____
move	_____
bark	_____
clean	_____
love	_____
jump	_____
wait	_____
miss	_____
dance	_____
smile	_____
hope	_____

Choose two past-tense verbs above. Write a sentences using each word.

1. _____

2. _____

0-7424-1802-2 *Building Grammar & Writing Skills*

Name _____ Date _____

In the Past

Some **verbs** end with a vowel and a consonant. To make these verbs past tense, double the consonant and add **ed.**

Example: drop = action now

drop**ped** = past action

Look at the pictures. Choose a word from the Word Box that goes with the picture. Write the word under the picture in past-tense form.

Word Box								
mop	pet	pop	bat	flap	stop	slip	hug	step

1.

_____

2.

_____

3.

_____

4.

_____

5.

_____

6.

_____

7.

_____

8.

_____

9.

_____

48

Name _____ Date _____

A Little Help

Sometimes verbs need help. Words like **will** and **can** are helping verbs. They come before the main verbs in a sentence. They "help" the main verbs tell what is going to happen.

Examples: She **can clean** the kitchen.
Tomorrow I **will go** to school.

Read the sentences. Circle the helping verbs. Underline the main verbs.

1. Next week I will sing in the school talent show.

2. Someday I will teach my dog to fetch.

3. After school Carter can come to my house to play.

4. Can you watch the movie with me tonight?

5. Amy will write her report after class.

6. The bird can fly now that its wing is healed.

7. The sun will rise tomorrow.

8. In January we can go to the mountains.

9. Patrick can run in the next race.

10. I will eat pizza for dinner.

0-7424-1802-2 *Building Grammar & Writing Skills*

Name _____ Date _____

Is, Am, Are

Is, am, and **are** belong to the "to be" family of verbs. They tell about "being" something now.

Examples: I **am** tall.
Summer **is** a warm season.
You **are** smart.

Read the sentences. Underline the "being" verbs.

1. Jenna is a great dancer.

2. We are going on vacation.

3. My grandparents are moving next door.

4. I am tired today.

5. The cat is sleeping in the sun.

Fill in the "being" verb to complete each sentence. Then draw a picture to go with it.

6. The flower _____ yellow.

7. I _____ happy.

8. Those puppies _____ playful.

   0-7424-1802-2 *Building Grammar & Writing Skills*

Name _____ Date _____

Was and Were

Was and **were** are also members of the "to be" verb family. They tell about "being" in the past.

Examples: I <u>**was**</u> tired last night.
You <u>**were**</u> playing well.
The leaves <u>**were**</u> red and yellow.

Read the story. Underline the verb that fits each sentence.

Last week Paul, Dina, and I went to the beach. We (was/were) so excited! The day (was/were) sunny and warm. I (was/were) collecting seashells when a huge wave crashed on the shore. Dina and I (was/were) soaked! The water (was/were) very cold. Paul (was/were) laughing. Another wave crashed ashore, and he (was/were) soaked, too! Then we (was/were) all laughing. After that, Dina and Paul (was/were) hungry, so we stopped to eat lunch. I (was/were) late getting home, but it (was/were) worth it. It (was/were) a great day!

0-7424-1802-2 *Building Grammar & Writing Skills*

Name _____ Date _____

Has, Have, Had

Have, has, and **had** are also members of the "to be" verb family. **Have** and **has** tell about actions happening now. **Had** tells about actions that happened in the past.

Examples: I **have** brown hair.
Jane **has** three sisters.
Last night we **had** turkey for dinner.

Write P next to sentences that tell about the **past.** Write **N** next to sentences that tell about **now.**

1. I have a pet rabbit. _____

2. Donna and her brother have freckles. _____

3. Joe had a hot fudge sundae yesterday. _____

4. Jennifer has a fear of spiders. _____

5. Do you have an extra pencil? _____

6. We had a lot of fun at the bowling alley. _____

7. My grandma had a horse when she was young. _____

8. I have a plan. _____

9. Pablo has lost a tooth. _____

10. The birds have beautiful feathers. _____

0-7424-1802-2 *Building Grammar & Writing Skills*

Name _____ Date _____

Match It!

Nouns and verbs work together in sentences. If the noun tells about one person, place, or thing, the verb has an **s** or **es** at the end.

Example: My brother **loves** to sing.
My sisters **love** to dance.

Read the sentences. Circle the correct verb that completes each sentence.

1. Izzy (drink   drinks) milk with her dinner.

2. Angela (bake   bakes) cookies with her mother.

3. Dad (drives   drive) me to school.

4. Eddie and his brother (share   shares) a bedroom.

5. Our team (wear   wears) red uniforms.

6. My grandparents (live   lives) next door.

7. The house (look   looks) old.

8. Can you (play   plays) the piano?

9. I (wash   washes) my hands before I eat.

10. Jeff (sit   sits) in the front row.

53

                      0-7424-1802-2 *Building Grammar & Writing Skills*

Name _____ Date _____

Ready for Review

Remember, nouns name a person, place, or thing. Verbs are action or "being" words. Color the balloons with nouns **purple.** Color the balloons with verbs **yellow.**

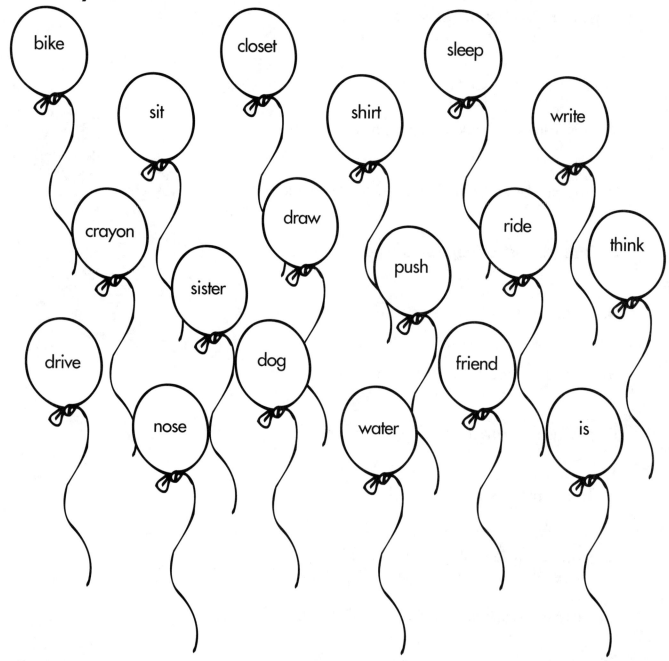

0-7424-1802-2 *Building Grammar & Writing Skills*

Name _____ Date _____

Pronoun Power

Pronouns take the place of nouns.

Examples:

<u>Corey</u> made cookies.   <u>The snow</u> is cold.   I called <u>**my parents**</u>.
<u>**He**</u> made cookies.   <u>**It**</u> is cold.   I called <u>**them**</u>.

Pronouns		
I	we	he
she	it	they
you	me	us
him	her	them

Read each pair of sentences. Complete the second sentence with a pronoun or pronouns from the box.

1. Wiley ran into the cabin.

_____ found his mittens.

2. Sherry takes ice-skating lessons.

She loves _____.

3. Randy and Marisa ate lunch outside.

Then _____ went back inside.

4. Cora told Shelby a joke.

_____ laughed at _____.

5. My mom rode on a sled with Randy.

_____ went with _____ many times.

6. Bobby and I each scored a goal.

The team cheered for _____.

7. My dad took his dog for a walk in

the snow. _____ walked for an hour.

8. Kerri and Tana built a huge snowman.

_____ named _____ Leroy.

55

0-7424-1802-2 *Building Grammar & Writing Skills*

Name _____ Date _____

All About Me

I and **me** are pronouns. Use **I** and **me** when you talk about yourself. Use **I** when you are doing the action (you are the **subject**). Use **me** when you are receiving the action (you are the **object**).

Example: <u>**I gave**</u> Tina the cupcakes.

Tina gave cupcakes <u>**to me**</u>.

Read the sentences. Circle the words that are doing the action. Underline the words that are receiving the action.

1. I gave a birthday present to Wendy.

2. Wendy gave her pencil to me.

3. Marcia and I bought ice-cream cones.

4. Jan went with Marcia and me.

5. Justin took a picture of me.

6. I took a picture of the mountains.

Write **I** or **me** to complete each sentence.

7. Colin and _____ helped with the dishes.

8. Mom made Gretchen and _____ sandwiches.

9. _____ like Laura.

10. Laura likes _____

11. Dad helped _____ with my homework.

12. _____ like to do homework.

56

Name _____ Date _____

It's All Mine

Some **pronouns** show that something "belongs" to someone or something.

Example: **My** sister is two years old.
Her hair is blonde.
Your pencil is broken.
This house is **ours.**
That bike is **his.**

Look at these "belonging" pronouns in the word jar. Read the story and underline the belonging pronouns. Then circle what each pronoun "belongs" to.

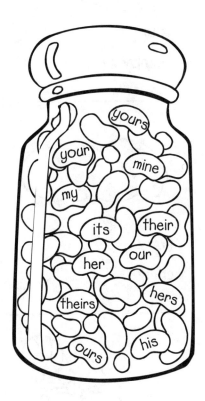

    Mrs. Wyatt's second-grade class had a science fair. Dylan made a volcano. His volcano had pretend lava. Sheri and Sue showed how to make sugar crystals. Their project was small. Lee grew a plant. He painted some of the leaves. "Your projects are all very good," Mrs. Wyatt said. "But their tags are all mixed up."

    "The plant is mine," said Lee.

    "I know the volcano is yours," Mrs. Wyatt told Dylan. "Which
project is yours?" she asked Sheri.

    "The crystal garden is ours," replied Sheri and Sue.

57

0-7424-1802-2 *Building Grammar & Writing Skills*

Name _____ Date _____

Describing Words

Adjectives are words that describe nouns. They may describe how something looks, sounds, tastes, smells, or feels.

Look at each picture and read the adjectives. Add one more adjective to describe the picture.

sour

bumpy

_____

stinky

old

_____

unhappy

loud

_____

fluffy

chilly

_____

striped

soft

_____

funny

goofy

_____

sweet

sticky

_____

sharp

round

_____

icy

wet

_____

0-7424-1802-2 *Building Grammar & Writing Skills*

Name _____ Date _____

Two Big, Round Blue Eyes

Some **adjectives** tell about number, size, shape, or color.

Read the sentences. Circle all the adjectives.
Then write each adjective in the correct column.

1. Three birds landed on a small branch.

2. Leah had five pink ribbons in her hair.

3. The tall square building is the library.

4. I ate two big helpings of ice cream.

5. The package had a wide yellow ribbon.

6. Rosa wore a round white hat.

7. One car had a flat tire.

8. The television screen had tiny squiggly lines.

9. There were six green apples in the bowl.

10. The picture was in an oval silver frame.

SIZE	SHAPE	COLOR	NUMBER

0-7424-1802-2 *Building Grammar & Writing Skills*

Name _____ Date _____

All These Adjectives

Some **adjectives** come after "being" verbs, like **am, is, are, was,** and **were.**
They describe what something is like or how it feels.

Unscramble each sentence and rewrite it on the line. Circle the adjective.

1. stories the scary were.

_____

2. hungry am I.

_____

3. thunder the loud was.

_____

4. trees were green the.

_____

5. elephant fat the is.

_____

6. excited are the children.

_____

7. birthday was Jessie on happy her.

_____

8. weather the yesterday cold was.

_____

9. light bright was the.

_____

10. am tired I.

_____

0-7424-1802-2 *Building Grammar & Writing Skills*

Name _____ Date _____

Comparing with Adjectives

Some **adjectives** compare things. When you compare two things, add **er** to the adjective. When you compare more than two things, add **est** to the adjective.

Example: My rat is **bigger** than yours.
My rat is the **biggest** of all.

Add **er** or **est** to the adjectives in parentheses to complete the sentences. Write them on the lines.

1. Eddie is _____ than Joe. (young)

2. The library is the _____ building in town. (tall)

3. Lakota is _____ than Midnight. (fast)

4. Ralph's flashlight is the _____. (bright)

5. Andra's hair is _____ than Madison's. (long)

6. Jordan can throw _____ than me. (hard)

7. Sam and Linita are the _____ in the class. (smart)

8. Our classroom is _____ than theirs. (cold)

9. Patti is the _____ athlete in the school. (great)

10. The cake is _____ than the pie. (sweet)

0-7424-1802-2 *Building Grammar & Writing Skills*

Name _____ Date _____

All About Adverbs

An **adverb** describes a verb. An adverb tells when, where, or how something happened.

Examples: Claire sings **<u>often</u>**. (when)
Claire sings **<u>here</u>**. (where)
Claire sings **<u>beautifully</u>**. (how)

Look at each picture. Then complete each sentence with a word from the correct word box.

Where

here, there, outside, over, behind, under, everywhere, up, around

When

weekly, later, yesterday, often, sometimes, today, now, soon, always

How

carefully, noisily, softly, slowly, hard, quickly, happily, loudly, quietly

1.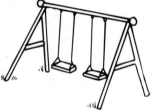

Carlos swings _____. (where)
Carlos swings _____. (when)
Carlos swings _____. (how)

3.

It rained _____. (where)
It rained _____. (when)
It rained _____. (how)

2.

The mouse ran _____. (where)
The mouse ran _____. (when)
The mouse ran _____. (how)

4.

Hayley draws pictures. (where)
Hayley draws pictures _____. (when)
Hayley draws pictures _____. (how)

0-7424-1802-2 *Building Grammar & Writing Skills*

Name _____ Date _____

Ready for Review

Read the sentences. Underline the adjectives in green. Circle the adverbs in red.

1. Our slow mail carrier delivered our mail late.

2. I ate the hot soup slowly.

3. The sneaky snake slithered quietly through the forest.

4. Angela often wrote long letters.

5. Darryl curled up under the warm blue blanket.

6. The new supermarket opens early.

7. Fluffy white snow drifted lazily.

8. Yesterday Denny baked a chocolate cake.

9. My older cousin Anna will be here soon.

10. Rebecca placed her pink umbrella behind the big door.

11. We ran quickly to the big museum before it closed.

12. She always writes the best papers in the class.

0-7424-1802-2 *Building Grammar & Writing Skills*

Name _____ Date _____

A, An, The

The words **a** and **an** are called **articles.**
They "introduce" nouns.

A introduces a noun that starts with a consonant.

I bought **a** pair of ice skates.

An introduces a noun that starts with a vowel.

You can use skates at **an** ice rink.

The introduces a noun that names a specific person, place, or thing.

The ice rink in our town is new.

Write **a** or **an** to introduce each noun.

1. _____ fish   2. _____wish

3. _____ mask   4. _____oven

5. _____ umbrella 6. _____wolf

7. _____ planet   8. _____arm

9. _____ oar   10. _____tooth

Underline the correct article to complete each sentence.

11. I went to (an/a) movie.

12. The hen laid (a/an) egg.

13. When (the/a) alarm clock rings, I get up.

14. My mom went to this school (a/the) long time ago.

15. This is (a/the) movie I want you to see.

64

Name _____ Date _____

Multiple Meanings

Some words can "play" different parts. They can be nouns, verbs, adjectives, or adverbs.

Read the sentences and look at the **bold** words. Underline the "part" that word is playing in the sentence. The first one is done for you.

1. Goose **down** is very warm. (<u>noun</u>/verb)
   Anisa walked **down** the hill. (<u>adverb</u>/adjective)

2. Let's **plan** a party. (noun/verb)
   We can write a **plan** on paper. (noun/verb)

3. The window locks with a small **hook**. (noun/verb)
   John was hoping to **hook** a fish. (noun/verb)

4. Do you know how to **fold** a napkin? (noun/verb)
   There is a **fold** in your book cover. (noun/verb)

5. I read the **end** of the book. (noun/verb)
   Please **end** your story. (noun/verb)

6. I bought my mom some **cut** flowers. (verb/adjective)
   Cut the string. (verb/adjective)

7. Put the **cover** on the pot. (noun/verb)
   Cover the birdcage. (noun/verb)

8. The water in the **well** is cold. (noun/adverb)
   You write **well**. (noun/adverb)

0-7424-1802-2 *Building Grammar & Writing Skills*

Name _____ Date _____

Crazy Compounds

Some words can be put together to make a new word. This new word is called a **compound word**.

Read each word list. See how many words you can put together to make compound words.

1. bath, room, bed, blue, bird (4 new words)

_____ _____ _____

_____

2. sun, rise, light, flash, house, dog (5 new words)

_____ _____ _____

_____ _____

3. sand, box, car, bag, shoe (4 new words)

_____ _____ _____

_____

4. pan, cake, cup, tea, pot, flower (5 new words)

_____ _____ _____

_____ _____

5. way, door, knob, hall, bell (4 new words)

_____ _____ _____

_____

0-7424-1802-2 *Building Grammar & Writing Skills*

Name _____ Date _____

Silly Synonyms

Synonyms are words with the same or almost the same meaning.

Examples: sleep, nap, snooze

Read the words under each picture. Cross out the word that does not belong.

 1. neat   tidy   sloppy   orderly

 2. cold   hot   chilly   icy

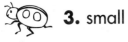 **3.** small   little   bug   tiny

 4. happy   glad   cheery   sad

 5. flower   tree   blossom   bud

 6. big   huge   gray   large

 7. shout   yell   scream   whisper

 8. laugh   cry   giggle   chuckle

    0-7424-1802-2 *Building Grammar & Writing Skills*

Name _____ Date _____

Observing Opposites

Antonyms are words that have opposite meanings.

Examples: clean—dirty; happy—sad; love—hate

Look at the pictures. Draw a line to match the opposites.

0-7424-1802-2 *Building Grammar & Writing Skills*

Name _____ Date _____

Sounds the Same

Some words sound alike, but they have different meanings.

Examples: hear—here; sea—see; I—eye

Circle the word that best completes each sentence.

1. Would you like to (meet   meat) my friend.

2. Gail wore a (blew   blue) dress.

3. My brother is (for   four) years old.

4. The (sun   son) helps plants make food.

5. (Wood   Would) you like some ice cream?

6. We (ate   eight) pizza for lunch.

7. I have a new (pear   pair) of shoes.

8. I don't (no   know) the answer.

9. It isn't polite to (stare   stair).

10. Can you tie a square (not   knot)?

0-7424-1802-2 *Building Grammar & Writing Skills*

Name _____ Date _____

There, Their, They're

There, their, and **they're** sound alike, but they have different meanings.
>   **There** is a "place" word—The book is over **there.**
>   **Their** is a "belonging" word—This is *their* house.
>   **They're** is a short way to write **they are**—*They're* always late.

Write **there, their,** or **they're** to correctly complete each sentence.

1. It was _____ when I looked.

2. _____ cookies are very tasty.

3. _____ students in Mr. Hsu's class.

4. Give _____ tickets to them.

5. _____ riding the roller coaster.

6. The roller coaster is over _____

7. We will go _____ for our vacation

8. Mom said _____ coming with us.

9. They have to pack _____ bags.

10. _____ pet pig is so cute!

70

Name _____ Date _____

Your and You're

Your and **you're** sound alike, but they have different meanings.
       Your is a belonging word—Is this **your** pig?
       You're is a short way to write **you are**—**You're** so lucky!

Write **your** or **you're** to correctly complete each sentence

1. _____ invited to my sleepover.

2. Please bring _____ sleeping bag.

3. _____ welcome to bring your dog.

4. _____ mom will drive you to my house.

5. You have to call _____ parents.

6. _____ going to love my new video game!

7. Is this game harder than _____ game?

8. I can tell _____ getting sleepy.

9. When is _____ bedtime?

10. Next time we will stay at _____ house.

71

Name _____ Date _____

Two, To, Too

Two, to, and **too** sound alike, but they have different meanings.

Two is a number word.

    Two birds sang.

To can come before a verb; it can also mean "toward."

    I want **to** go **to** the zoo.

Too can mean "also" or "more than enough."

    Wyatt wants to go *too*, but he is *too* tired.

Read each sentence. If **two, to,** or **too** is used correctly, color the picture. If the word is used incorrectly, cross it out and write the correct word above it.

I.

Gabriel is going too catch the ball.

2.

It is too windy to go outside.

3.

There are two frogs in the pond.

4.

Monkeys love two eat bananas.

     0-7424-1802-2 *Building Grammar & Writing Skills*

Name _____ Date _____

Rhyme Time

Rhyming words end with the same sound.

Examples: clip—ship; stop—pop; tall—crawl

Draw lines to connect the three words that rhyme. The first one is done for you.

1. pet ----------------------- wet		told
2. light	sweet	played
3. mold	made	weed
4. look	sold	treat
5. read	said	get
6. meat	seed	crow
7. sew	tight	took
8. tree	book	head
9. grade	me	bright
10. red	blow	sea

0-7424-1802-2 *Building Grammar & Writing Skills*

Name _____ Date _____

Writing Rhymes

Use words from the Word Box to complete the rhymes. Draw a picture to go with each rhyme.

Word Box

chair	light	bake
mouse	broom	zoo

1. To make a cake,

You have to _____

2. In Grandma's house

There is a _____!

3. When I sleep at night,

I turn off the _____

4. My Aunt Lou

Works at the _____

5. To clean my room,

I'll need a _____

6. I'll sit down there

In that green _____

0-7424-1802-2 *Building Grammar & Writing Skills*

Name _____ Date _____

Blooming Words

A **contraction** is two words put together. But some letters are left out.
An **apostrophe** takes the place of the missing letters.

Examples: can not   can ~~not~~   can't
           she is,   she ~~is~~   she's

Match each set of two words to its contractions by
coloring the flowers the same color.

I'm, it's, he's, we are, she'll, you're, aren't, she will, she's, was not, I am, you are, isn't, is not, she is, wasn't, are not, he is, it is, we're

   0-7424-1802-2 *Building Grammar & Writing Skills*

Name _____ Date _____

Creating Contractions

Read the sentences. Use the words under the lines to write a contraction to complete each sentence.

1. We _____ sit on the park bench until the paint is dry.
       can not

2. Becky _____ feeling well.
       is not

3. _____ run near the pool.
    Do not

4. Paula and her brother _____ at the football game.
       were not

5. _____ seven years old.
    I am

6. _____ love this new game.
    You will

7. Bishop said _____ happy to go back to school.
      he is

8. Brenda wants to know if _____ finished music class.
       you have

9. _____ snowing!
    it is

10. Dinner _____ be ready until later.
    will not

0-7424-1802-2 *Building Grammar & Writing Skills*

Name _____ Date _____

Simple Subjects

The **naming part** (subject) of a sentence tells who or what the sentence is about.

Example: <u>Pablo and I</u> want to learn how to snowboard.

Read the sentences. Underline the "naming part" of each sentence.

1. The trees on Ames Street are very tall.

2. Jessie and Arlo had hamburgers for lunch.

3. The old town library is being painted.

4. A tall woman was carrying a flag.

5. A large dust cloud rose in the air.

6. Brie laughed until she cried.

Write a "naming part" for each sentence.

7. _____ ran under the bridge.

8. _____ are too big for him.

9. _____ has a long, fluffy tail.

10. _____ filled a bucket with water.

11. _____ ran fast.

12. _____ jumped over the fence.

77

Name _____ Date _____

Awesome Action

The **action part** (predicate) of a sentence tells what happened.

Example: A duck <u>landed in the swimming pool.</u>

Underline the "action part" of each sentence.

1. The big green crocodile gobbled up a fish.

2. Ms. Angelo's class planted a garden.

3. The boy carved the huge pumpkin.

4. The baker rolled out the dough.

5. Stephen spilled milk on his new sweater.

6. The gray whale flipped its tail in the water.

Write an "action part" for each sentence.

7. The yellow ball _____

8. My kitten _____

9. The ice-cream man _____

10. Ray and Risa _____

11. A big wind _____

12. The dog down the street _____

78

Name _____ Date _____

Complete Sentences

A **complete sentence** begins with a capital letter. It has a naming part (subject) and an action part (predicate).

Look at each picture. Choose a naming part and action part from the lists below. Then write a complete sentence under each picture.

Naming Part

Mrs. Bell's dog

The man in the black shirt

A flock of birds

My grandfather

When I was five,

The cowboy

Action Part

can play the violin.

flew over the park.

wore fancy boots.

I visited Australia.

begs on its hind legs!

ran for the bus.

1. _____

2. _____

3. _____

4. _____

5. _____

6. _____

0-7424-1802-2 *Building Grammar & Writing Skills*

Name _____ Date _____

Incomplete Sentences

Read the story. Underline eight incomplete sentences.

Gabe wanted to get home early. His Uncle Ted was coming to visit. Used to live in Montana. Uncle Ted told great stories. Gabe ran faster. When he raced up the steps. There was Uncle Ted. He was eating a sandwich.

"Hi, Uncle Ted," Gabe said happily.

"Hi Gabe," his uncle answered. Been waiting for you. We are going to go camping."

"Hooray!" Gabe cried. "I'll get my sleeping bag."

They packed food and warm clothes. Packed plenty of it. They drove to the campsite. A river nearby. They set up the tent and built a fire. Uncle Ted told stories about Montana. About a big black bear. When Gabe was sleepy, he curled up in his sleeping bag. As he fell asleep he thought he heard a bear. In the morning.

"I dreamed about a bear," Gabe told his uncle.

"Your dream left footprints," said Uncle Ted. Near the tent.

"Wow," Gabe said with a smile. "Now *I'll* have a story to tell."

0-7424-1802-2 *Building Grammar & Writing Skills*

Writing Strategies: Sentences

Name _____ Date _____

It's Telling

A **telling sentence** gives information. It begins
with a capital letter and ends with a period. **(.)**

Read the sentences. Circle the letters that should be
capitals. Put a period at the end of each sentence.

1. amber woke up early

2. it was snowing

3. she dressed in warm clothes

4. lin and tyrone built a snowman

5. karen loves hot chocolate

6. the black dog played in the snow

7. allie made snow angels

8. the pond is frozen

9. haley is a good ice skater

10. alex lost her fuzzy green mittens

Write two telling sentences about what you did today.

_____

_____

Published by Instructional Fair. Copyright protected.   0-7424-1802-2 *Building Grammar & Writing Skills*

Name _____ Date _____

Asking Questions

An **asking sentence** asks a question. It begins with a capital letter and ends with a question mark. **(?)**

Read the sentences. Choose an asking word from the question mark to complete each sentence. End each with a question mark.

1. _____ missed the bus

2. _____ did Elisa leave

3. _____ old are you

4. _____ is Mia wearing your sweater

5. _____ is in that box

6. _____ did you do that

7. _____ did Garret say

8. _____ did you hurt your arm

Write two asking sentences about something you want to learn to do.

_____

_____

0-7424-1802-2 *Building Grammar & Writing Skills*

Name _____ Date _____

Change It Around

Sometimes you can move the words around in a sentence to change its meaning.

Look at each picture and read the sentence. Rewrite the sentence so it matches the picture. Remember to capitalize the first word and add a period.

I.

The chair is sitting on the kitten.

_____

2.

The water is in the fish.

_____

3.

The baseball threw the boy.

_____

4.

Greta spread bread on jam.

_____

5.

Candace found toy bears under her bed.

_____

6.

The player yelled as the bases ran around the crowd.

_____

0-7424-1802-2 *Building Grammar & Writing Skills*

Name _____ Date _____

Ready for Review

Read the sentences. Cross out two incomplete sentences. Write **A** next to asking sentences. Write **T** next to telling sentences.
Add a period or question mark.

1. Soledad painted a picture of her cat _____

2. Do you like strawberries _____

3. Scott plays piano well _____

4. Under the tree near the river _____

5. What is your address _____

6. March is a windy month _____

7. What time is it _____

8. The girl with the brown hair _____

9. Are you sure _____

10. Stephanie has a rock collection _____

84

   0-7424-1802-2 *Building Grammar & Writing Skills*

Name _____ Date _____

Combining Sentences

If two sentences have the same idea, you can combine them. You can join two sentences with the words **or, and,** or **but.**

Examples: Jonah likes cherries. Jonah likes grapes.
Jonah likes cherries **and** grapes.

Leslie can't sing. Leslie can't dance.
Leslie can't sing **or** dance.

Allen likes books. Allen doesn't like movies.
Allen likes books **but** not movies.

Read each sentence pair. Use **or, and,** or **but** to join the sentences together.

1. Juan found a cricket in his backyard. Juan found a ladybug.

_____

2. Britney likes math. Britney likes art.

_____

3. We might have pizza for lunch. We might have salad for lunch.

_____

4. I ran to school. I was late.

_____

5. Dennis went to Ann's party. Tony went to Ann's party.

_____

6. I saw you. I didn't hear what you said.

_____

85

Name _____ Date _____

The Main Idea

The **main idea** is the most important idea in a paragraph or story.

Look at each picture. Underline the sentence that tells the main idea.

1.

Jessica's cat loves milk.

Jessica spilled the milk.

Jessica is clumsy.

2.

Grandpas are good at fishing.

There are lots of fish in the river.

Grandpa helped the boy fish.

3.

Greta and Tim painted Buddy's doghouse.

The dog was bored.

Painting is hard work.

4.

Sally Squirrel is a good painter.

Sally Squirrel paints acorns.

Sally Squirrel's favorite food is acorns.

0-7424-1802-2 *Building Grammar & Writing Skills*

Name _____ Date _____

Important Ideas

The **main idea** is the most important idea in a paragraph or story.

Read each story. Underline the main idea. Then rewrite it on the line below.

1. Carl is both sad and excited because it is his first day at a new school. He doesn't have any friends. He would like to make a friend. He sees another boy who has dropped his notebook. The boy picks up the papers. He doesn't notice a paper behind a tree. Carl gets the paper and gives it to the boy. It is a homework paper. The boy is very happy. He asks Carl to sit with him at lunch.

_____

2. Maggie wants to surprise her dad for his birthday. She made him a card. She got up early and made a special breakfast of toast and orange juice. She brought it in on a tray. Dad was so happy!

_____

3. Kevin is excited. Today is the day he will get his fish tank. He has wanted one for a long time. He read everything he could about goldfish. He knows exactly what he wants. His mom told him they could go as soon as he finished his homework.

_____

0-7424-1802-2 *Building Grammar & Writing Skills*

Name _____ Date _____

Reading a Recipe

Anna wants to make blueberry muffins, but the recipe is all mixed up! The muffins won't turn out unless she follows the steps in order.

Number the steps from **1** to **10** to put them in order.

_____ Let muffins cool.

_____ Then add eggs, milk, and oil.

_____ Put fresh blueberries in last.

_____ Put flour and sugar in bowl.

_____ Pour batter in muffin pan.

_____ Put muffins on plate and serve.

_____ Get out ingredients.

_____ Put muffin pan in oven.

_____ Bake for 30 minutes.

_____ Stir batter until it is all mixed together.

0-7424-1802-2 *Building Grammar & Writing Skills*

Name _____ Date _____

Story Order

Stories are written in order. The sentences in this story
are all mixed up! Write the numbers **1** to **10** to
put them in order.

_____ Ian walked Sparky down the street and to the park.

_____ Sparky splashed into the water.

_____ "I know what we are doing next," Ian said. "You need a bath."

_____ They walked to the pond at the center of the park.

_____ Ian clipped Sparky's new red leash on her collar.

_____ Sparky pranced out of the pond covered in mud.

_____ She barked and pulled at her leash until it slipped from Ian's hand.

_____ Sparky saw a flock of wild ducks in the water.

_____ Ian decided to go for a walk with his dog, Sparky.

_____ The ducks quacked, flapped, and flew away.

89

0-7424-1802-2 *Building Grammar & Writing Skills*

Name_____ Date _____

Organize the Animals

Group the animals that go together. Write the name of each animal under the correct title.

tiger

elephant

dog

cat

giraffe

Wild Animals	Farm Animals	Pets

chicken

hippo

cow

pig

sheep

90

0-7424-1802-2 *Building Grammar & Writing Skills*

Name _____ Date _____

What Doesn't Belong?

Beth spent the day at the beach. Cross out one thing in each row that Beth would not see at the beach.

1.

2.

3.

4.

5.

91

Name _____ Date _____

Perfect Paragraph

A **paragraph** is made up of sentences. The sentences are about one main idea.

Read the sentences. Circle each sentence that might be in a paragraph about Thanksgiving.

1. Families gather for dinner.

2. I was in a play in first grade.

3. It takes place on the third Thursday in November.

4. Many trees lose leaves in the fall.

5. Pilgrims and Native Americans celebrated the first Thanksgiving.

6. The turkey is a symbol of the holiday.

7. November is the eleventh month.

8. The meal may end with pumpkin pie.

9. It is a national holiday.

10. Valentine's Day is in February.

92

0-7424-1802-2 *Building Grammar & Writing Skills*

Name _____ Date _____

Tricky Topics

The **topic sentence** is the main idea of a paragraph. It tells what the paragraph is about. It is usually the first or second sentence.

Read each paragraph. Underline the topic sentence. Then rewrite the topic sentence on the line.

1. My grandfather knows a lot about horses. He is from Wyoming. When Grandpa was five years old, he rode a horse for the first time. He learned to ride from his dad. He learned to rope, too. Grandpa was in a rodeo when he was a teenager. He won a blue ribbon. Grandpa said the most important thing about riding is being friends with your horse.

_____

2. I usually like school. Yesterday I had a tough day. Nothing went right. I forgot my homework. I spilled paint on my teacher's desk. I dropped my lunch on the floor. Mrs. James called on me, and I didn't know the answer. She said that was okay. Everybody has a tough day once in a while. My mom made my favorite dinner last night. She said today would be better. She was right!

_____

0-7424-1802-2 *Building Grammar & Writing Skills*

Name _____ Date _____

In the End

Every **paragraph** has an ending sentence. It usually "sums up" the ideas in the paragraph.

1. Read the paragraph. Underline the best ending sentence.

My dad and I like to fly kites together. We each have our own kite. Dad's kite looks like a big blue box. My kite looks like an eagle.
We go to a big field in Brenner Park to fly our kites. Today there is a light wind.

The wind means rain is coming.

My dog likes Brenner Park.

The eagle is an American symbol.

Today would be a good day to fly our kites.

My dad's favorite color is blue.

2. Read the paragraph. Then write your own ending sentence.

Last week our class visited City Hall. We rode on a bus to Main Street. A nice man met our bus and showed us around City Hall. We got to meet the mayor. She was very nice. We _____

_____.

0-7424-1802-2 *Building Grammar & Writing Skills*

Name _____ Date _____

Beginning, Middle, and End

A **paragraph** has a beginning, middle, and end. Draw three pictures to tell a short story about a favorite family event, like a birthday party, holiday, or vacation.

Write your story in three sentences. Tell what happened first, next, and last.

Beginning

_____

_____

Middle

_____

_____

End

_____

_____

95

0-7424-1802-2 *Building Grammar & Writing Skills*

Name _____ Date _____

Finding Facts

Brent is writing a report about the solar system. He needs lots of facts to complete his report.

Read this paragraph about the solar system. Then look at the sentences below. Write **Y** if the information was in the paragraph. Write **N** if it was not in the paragraph.

The Solar System

The solar system is the sun and everything that moves around it. There are nine known planets in the solar system. The planet closest to the sun is Mercury. The planet furthest from the sun is Pluto. Pluto is also the smallest planet. The largest is Jupiter. Most of the planets have moons. Moons are natural bodies that circle around a planet. Earth is the third planet from the sun. Earth has one moon. Some of the other objects in the solar system are comets and asteroids.

1. There are nine planets in the solar system. _____

2. There are more than 100 moons in the solar system. _____

3. Jupiter is the largest planet. _____

4. Most of the planets have moons. _____

5. My sister went to space camp last summer. _____

6. Pluto is the smallest planet. _____

7. Pluto is the furthest planet from the sun. _____

8. Asteroids are like big space rocks. _____

9. Mercury is the closest planet to the sun. _____

10. Mars is smaller than Earth. _____

0-7424-1802-2 *Building Grammar & Writing Skills*

Name _____ Date _____

Clever Clues

You can use clues from what you read to find information.

These students each wrote a report. Use the clues to figure out who wrote each report. Write the author's name under the correct title.

Space	Mountains	Pioneers	Mexico	Oceans	The Rain Forest
By: _____	By: _____	By: _____	By: _____	By: _____	By: _____

 Corey   Rosa   Mateo   Ray   Taylor   Marcus

1. Corey likes stories of the old west.

2. Marcus is learning to speak Spanish.

3. Rosa doesn't like heights.

4. Mateo interviewed an astronaut.

5. Taylor likes to grow plants.

6. Ray has a rock collection.

7. Rosa is a good swimmer.

8. Marcus interviewed his aunt in Acapulco.

9. Taylor loves animals.

10. Ray can climb a rock wall.

0-7424-1802-2 *Building Grammar & Writing Skills*

Name _____ Date _____

Table of Contents

A **table of contents** is a list of the topics that can be found in a book. It can help you find information.

Read the table of contents for this book on weather. Then answer the questions below.

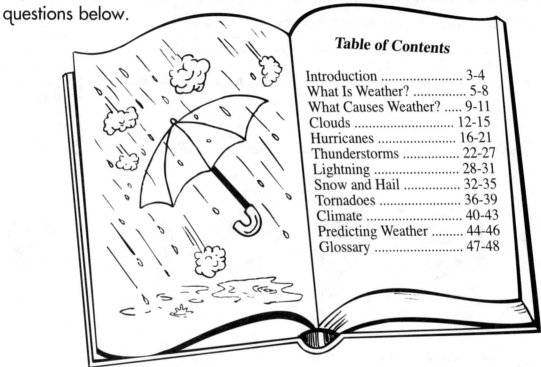

Table of Contents

Introduction 3-4
What Is Weather? 5-8
What Causes Weather? 9-11
Clouds 12-15
Hurricanes 16-21
Thunderstorms 22-27
Lightning 28-31
Snow and Hail 32-35
Tornadoes 36-39
Climate 40-43
Predicting Weather 44-46
Glossary 47-48

1. Which pages tell about tornadoes? _____

2. Which pages tell how to predict the weather? _____

3. Which pages might have safety tips about hurricanes? _____

4. Would this book help with a report on desert animals? _____

5. What will you learn about on page 29? _____

6. Where should you look for the introduction? _____

7. Where can you find the meaning of a new word? _____

8. Which pages tell about clouds? _____

9. What will you learn about on page 40? _____

10. How many pages are in the book? _____

0-7424-1802-2 *Building Grammar & Writing Skills*

Name _____ Date _____

In the Index

An **index** lists people, places, and things that can be found in a book. It lists them in ABC order. The index is at the back of a book.

Read this index from a book about the rain forest. Then answer the questions below.

Africa 11, 33, 57	gorilla 11, 37
Amazon 9, 33	howler monkey 19
Australia 13, 57	insects 5, 19, 29, 35, 39
bamboo 13	jaguar 9
bird-eating spider 9	jungle floor 5, 15, 23
birds 41	leeches 45
canopy 5, 19, 23, 27, 41, 43	reptiles 47
capuchin monkey 41	spider monkey 9
Central America 59	three-toed sloth 19, 41
chimpanzee 37	understory 5
giant water lily 29	vampire bat 31

1. Which pages tell about insects? _____

2. Does this book tell about monkeys? _____

3. What can you learn about on page 9? _____

4. Does this book tell about Africa? _____

5. Can you learn about elephants in this book? _____

6. Is page 11 about the Amazon? _____

7. Which page tells about the vampire bat? _____

8. Which three animals are on page 41? _____

9. Which page might tell about snakes? _____

10. Does this book tell about plants? _____

0-7424-1802-2 *Building Grammar & Writing Skills*

Name _____ Date _____

Using a Dictionary

You can look up new words in a **dictionary.** The words are in ABC order.

Hint: When putting words in ABC order, start with the first letter, then the second letter, and so on.

Write each group of words in the order you would find them in the dictionary.

1. cat   fish   bib   dish

_____   _____   _____   _____

2. kettle   ice   house   jump

_____   _____   _____   _____

3. oar   mop   nap   map

_____   _____   _____   _____

4. pour   peach   pumpkin   pair

_____   _____   _____   _____

5. bunch   apple   egg   coal

_____   _____   _____   _____

6. zebra   yellow   zoo   umbrella

_____   _____   _____   _____

7. whistle   vase   vote   whale

_____   _____   _____   _____

8. grape   face   fall   icicle

_____   _____   _____   _____

     0-7424-1802-2 *Building Grammar & Writing Skills*

Name _____ Date _____

Guiding Words

At the top of every dictionary page there are two **guide words.** These are the first and last words on the page. All the other words fall between, in ABC order.

Write the words from the Word Box on the dictionary page. Two words do not belong between the guide words. Cross them out.

Word Box					
market	mare	mass	mask	mascot	mat
margin	make	mark	mash	marsh	marine

march   mast

_____   _____

_____   _____

_____   _____

_____   _____

_____   _____

0-7424-1802-2 *Building Grammar & Writing Skills*

Name _____ Date _____

Organize an Outline

An **outline** can help you put your ideas in order. Look at
the subjects in the outline. Write the words from the
Word Box under the correct subjects.

Word Box			
July	icicles	chicks	swimming
Thanksgiving	ice cream	November	flowers
snowman	red leaves	January	May

1. Winter

    A. _____

    B. _____

    C. _____

2. Spring

    A. _____

    B. _____

    C. _____

3. Summer

    A. _____

    B. _____

    C. _____

4. Spring

    A. _____

    B. _____

    C. _____

0-7424-1802-2 *Building Grammar & Writing Skills*

Name _____ Date _____

Writing a Report

A **fact** is information that most people believe is true. When you write a report, you need to include facts.

Unscramble this list of items where you might look to find facts for a report. Write the words on the lines. **Hint:** You can find the words by the pencil if you need help.

1. braryil _____

2. enycpedlcoia _____

3. gamanize _____

4. ookb _____

5. ntreInet _____

6. eacerht _____

7. sceinistt _____

8. seumum _____

9. tleevisnoi _____

Use items listed above to answer the questions about these animals.

Lion _____ **African Elephant Caribou**

10. Where does it live? _____

11. What does it eat? _____

103

0-7424-1802-2 *Building Grammar & Writing Skills*

Name _____ Date _____

Dear Friend

Sending a letter can be fun! Answer the questions below. Then write your letter.

I would like to write to _____

I would like to tell this person about _____

and _____.

I would like to ask this person about _____

_____.

Now, write your letter below.

Date _____

Dear _____,

_____

_____

_____

_____

_____

Your friend,

_____

Name _____ Date _____

The Story of Me

Some people write stories about their own lives. You can, too!
Fill in the information below, and you will have ideas for a story about you!

My name is _____

My favorite game is _____

I like to eat _____

My friends are _____

My family members are _____

What I like about school is _____

I am very good at _____

I would like to learn to _____

I laugh when _____

My pet is _____

When I grow up, I would like to _____

What I like best about me is _____

Write a story about you on a separate piece of paper. Use the information above.
If you wish, add more details, and give your story a title.

0-7424-1802-2 *Building Grammar & Writing Skills*

Name _____ Date _____

In My Journal

A journal is a book that you write in every day. You can write whatever you want. You can write what you do or what you think.

Think about what you did today. Write three things on this journal page.

My Journal

_____

_____

_____

_____

_____

_____

_____

_____

_____

_____

_____

_____

0-7424-1802-2 *Building Grammar & Writing Skills*

Name _____ Date _____

Write It Right

There are **22 mistakes** in this paragraph. Circle each mistake, and then write
it correctly.

Lorenzo couldnt wait to go to the book fair at his school. Evrey year there was a
guessing jar Lorenzo was sure that he could guess the write number.

"the prize is a basket of
books, he told his friend bryan.
"I know i will win. All I have to
do is guess. Are you going to
enter."

"I'll try," Bryan said.
after school Lorenzo went to the
fair. he found the guessing jar
and tried to count all the marbles

inside. He wrote his guess on a entry slip. He crossed his fingerz and dropped the
slip into the entry box.

The next day lorenzo received a telephone call
it is for you," his mom said with a smile. Lorenzo listened to the caller and
then he smiled two.

"I won " he shouted. Now all I have to do is read all them books."

0-7424-1802-2 *Building Grammar & Writing Skills*

Name _____ Date _____

Finding Ideas

Story ideas can come from lots of places. Sometimes you just need to sit and think, and write notes about your thoughts.

Look at the pictures below. Write four words about each picture. Choose one picture and write a story about it. Use your words in your story.

_____   _____   _____

_____   _____   _____

_____   _____   _____

_____   _____   _____

Title of Story: _____

_____

_____

_____

_____

_____

0-7424-1802-2 *Building Grammar & Writing Skills*

Name _____ Date _____

Map a Story

Look at the pictures. Write a sentence or two describing what is happening in each picture.

_____

_____

_____

_____

_____

_____

On another piece of paper, copy your sentences. Number them in order. Then fill in details about what you think is taking place in between what you see in the pictures. When you are finished, you will have a story map!

0-7424-1802-2 *Building Grammar & Writing Skills*

Name _____ Date _____

Create a Character

Characters are the people or animals in a story. Draw a picture of a character you would like to tell a story about. Answer the questions about your character.

What is your character's name? _____

Where was your character born? _____

What are your character's favorite things to do? _____

What is your character's least favorite thing to do? _____

What makes your character happy? _____

What makes your character sad? _____

What scares your character? _____

What is your character's family like? _____

Who are your character's friends? _____

0-7424-1802-2 *Building Grammar & Writing Skills*

Name _____ Date _____

Create a Place

A **setting** is where a story takes place.

Imagine a place on another planet. Draw a picture of your setting. Then answer the questions under the drawing.

What is your planet called? _____

Who lives there? _____

Who rules the planet? _____

Imagine a fantasy forest where fairies and a family of magical bunnies live.

What is the name of your fantasy forest? _____

What is the most special thing about it? _____

What will happens in the forest at night? _____

0-7424-1802-2 *Building Grammar & Writing Skills*

Name _____ Date _____

Point of View

Look at what is happening in the picture. Each character has a different idea about what happened. Answer the questions.

Do you think the boy who fell off the bike is having a good day? Write about what happened from his point of view.

_____

_____

_____

Do you think the boy who got the ice cream is having a good day? Write about what happened from his point of view.

_____

_____

_____

How do you think the ice-cream man feels?

_____

_____

What do you think the girl should do?

_____

_____

0-7424-1802-2 *Building Grammar & Writing Skills*

Name _____ Date _____

What Comes Next?

Look at the picture. Then read the three sentences below.
Underline the sentence that tells what you think will happen next.

1. The boy will pick up the book and give it back to the girl.

2. The girl will drop all of her books and scold the dog.

3. The dog will grab the book and run away with it.

Look at each picture. Write what you think will happen next.

_____

_____

_____

_____

_____

_____

0-7424-1802-2 *Building Grammar & Writing Skills*

Name _____ Date _____

Tell a Story

A **story** usually has characters, a setting, and a beginning, middle, and end. The characters usually have some kind of problem they need to solve.

Read this story then answer the questions.

      Tatiana was not happy about her teddy bear tea party. No guests had arrived.

      "I'm sure I wrote one o'clock on the invitations," she said aloud to her cat, Jeremy. "No one is here, and it's almost three!"

      Tatiana had planned everything so well. There was party music and balloons. The table was set for four girls and four bears. She had snacks and a big plate of chocolate chip cookies. Her teddy bear was wearing a fancy blue bow.

      "The invitations were even shaped like teddy bears," she said to Jeremy. "Like this." She held up a stack of cute cutout teddy bears. "Oh no," Tatiana cried. "These are the invitations!"

1. Who is the main character? _____

2. Name another character. _____

3. Where does the story take place? _____

4. What is the problem? _____

5. What was the answer? _____

Write you own ending to the story. _____

_____

_____

      0-7424-1802-2 *Building Grammar & Writing Skills*

Name _____ Date _____

Painting with Words

Some times you can "paint a picture" with words. Read each sentence and look at
the picture. Then use some of the words to rewrite a sentence that "paints" a
better picture.

Grandma read a book.
(favorite, boy, sleepy, softly, lap)

_____

_____

The wind blew.
(strong, rain, girl, wet, umbrella)

_____

_____

The monkeys played.
(happy, funny, swung, games, branch)

_____

_____

Tara held the kitten.
(fuzzy, soft, cuddled, petted, striped)

_____

_____

Name _____ Date _____

Amazing Myths

How did the leopard get spots? How did the rabbit get long ears? **Myths** tell stories about how things came to be. Myths aren't really true!

Read the story. Then circle the title that fits.

Why Some Dogs Have Floppy Ears

Long ago, all of the animals of the land planned a surprise party for the king. The dog was the king's best friend. The animals thought he might not keep the secret. When they talked about the party, they folded down the dog's ears so he couldn't hear. "It's a surprise," they would say. The party was a big success. The dog loved being surprised. To this day, many dogs keep their ears down. They are hoping that someone is planning a surprise party for them!

Why Some Dogs Have Floppy Ears

Why Dogs Can Hear Better Than Humans

How Dogs Became Pets

To write a myth, you need to use your imagination! Choose one of these titles and write a myth about it.

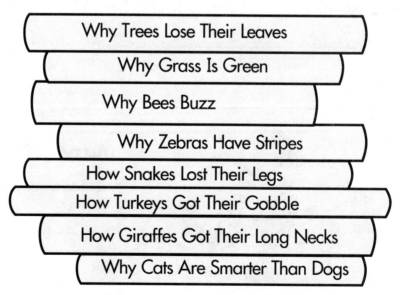

Why Trees Lose Their Leaves

Why Grass Is Green

Why Bees Buzz

Why Zebras Have Stripes

How Snakes Lost Their Legs

How Turkeys Got Their Gobble

How Giraffes Got Their Long Necks

Why Cats Are Smarter Than Dogs

0-7424-1802-2 *Building Grammar & Writing Skills*

Name _____ Date _____

Fun Fairy Tales

Fairy tales are made-up stories with magical characters, villains, heroes, and a happy ending. Anything can happen in a fairy tale! Animals can talk, brooms can walk, people can fly, and more!

Example: Main character: Cinderella
Villain: wicked stepmother
Problem: going to the ball
Magic: fairy godmother
Happy ending: Cinderella marries the prince

Choose one item from each list. Then answer the questions to start your own fairy tale!

Main Character: prince, princess, fairy, elf, unicorn, lost child
Villain: king or queen, witch or wizard, troll, gnome, monster
Magic: ring, wand, fairy, doll, animal, hat, shoes

What is your main character's problem? _____

_____

How does your character use magic to help? _____

_____

How does your character solve the problem? _____

_____

What is the happy ending? _____

_____

Write your fairy tale on a separate piece of paper.

117

Name _____ Date _____

Too Tall Tales

A **tall tale** is a story about someone who did something incredible, which has been handed down through history. As the story is retold, its events become more and more exaggerated.

Read this tall tale.

Gina Capola could make anything grow. If she planted an apple seed, an apple tree would grow by morning. The apples would peel themselves and jump into the nearest pie shell. If she planted cotton seeds, sweaters would spring up overnight. One day, Gina planted a kernel of corn. It grew and grew. People came from all over the state to see it. It grew so big that Gina opened a café inside of it. She served the best cornbread in the state!

Now, it's your turn to write a tall tale! Answer these questions to plan your story, then write it on a separate piece of paper.

1. Choose a tall tale hero. Think of someone who is strong, smart, brave, or athletic.

_____

2. Exaggerate your hero's talents. Make him or her bigger or stronger or faster or smarter than anyone else!

_____

_____

_____

3. Create an adventure for your hero. Once again, exaggerate! This cannot happen in real life.

_____

_____

_____

0-7424-1802-2 *Building Grammar & Writing Skills*

Name _____ Date _____

Story Starters

Story starters help a writer get ideas for stories. Sometime a picture or photo is a good story starter.

Look at the picture. Answer the questions, then write a short story about your ideas.

What are the names of the boy and girl?

_____

What does the message say?

_____

_____

Who or what is the shadow in the cave?

_____

_____

Write your story on a separate piece of paper.

Name _____ Date _____

More Story Starters

Read the story starters. Choose one story starter. Then write your story on a separate piece of paper. Draw a picture to go with it.

Richie was at the library looking for something to write his book report about. "I can help you," a tiny voice called from the shelves. "Where are you?" Randy asked in surprise. He pulled the book from the shelf. As he opened the pages . . .

Kayley looked at the 20-dollar bill in her hand. "I found it," she said aloud. "I wonder who it belongs to." Her friend, Teena, looked over her shoulder. "Wow! Twenty dollars! Let's go shopping!" Kayley didn't know what to do . . .

Troy was always playing tricks on his two sisters, Beth and Belinda. On day, Beth whispered to Belinda, "I have a great idea about how to play a trick on Troy." She opened her hand and showed Belinda what she was holding. "Oh my," Belinda giggled. "This is going to be so funny."

0-7424-1802-2 *Building Grammar & Writing Skills*

Name _____ Date _____

Write a Cinquain

A **cinquain** is a poem with five lines.

- **Line 1** has one word—the subject of the poem.
- **Line 2** has two words—they describe the subject.
- **Line 3** has three words—they include action.
- **Line 4** has four or five words—a thought about the subject.
- **Line 5** has the same word as line 1, or another word that means the same thing.

Read the sample. Then write a cinquain about one of the subjects below.

Party

Fun, noisy
Playing, eating, laughing
A time to be together
Celebrate

SCHOOL
FAVORITE HOLIDAY
LOVE

WINTER
SISTER/BROTHER
ICE CREAM

_____

_____

_____

_____

_____

Name _____ Date _____

Write a Diamante

A **diamante** poem doesn't have to rhyme. It has seven lines, and it changes its subject right in the middle of the poem!

- **Line 1** has one word—subject #1.
- **Line 2** has two words—they describe subject #1.
- **Line 3** has three words—they include action about subject #1.
- **Line 4** has four nouns—two about subject #1; two about subject #2
- **Line 5** has three words—they include action about subject #2
- **Line 6** has two words—they describe subject #2.
- **Line 7** has one word—subject #2.

Read the sample. Then write a diamante poem about winter and summer.

Dog
Furry, happy
Running, leaping, playing
Yip, bark, meow, purr
Grooming, napping, hunting
Soft, graceful
Cat

Winter–Summer

Winter

_____

_____

_____

_____

_____

_____

_____

Summer

0-7424-1802-2 *Building Grammar & Writing Skills*

Name _____ Date _____

Write Haiku

Haiku is a very old form of poetry from Japan. It does not have to rhyme. It has three lines. Each line should have a certain number of word parts called "syllables."

- **Line 1** has five syllables.
- **Line 2** has seven syllables.
- **Line 3** has five syllables.

Read the sample. Then write haiku poems about two of the subjects below.

Saturday is great.
I play and rest think and dream.
The weekend is mine.

FAVORITE SPORT	**KITTENS**	**FARM**
GRANDPARENT	**HAMBURGERS**	**BEST FRIEND**
ROSES	**CARNIVAL**	**HOME**

0-7424-1802-2 *Building Grammar & Writing Skills*

Name _____ Date _____

Time to Rhyme

Some poetry rhymes. Read the poem and finish the last line with a word that rhymes.

I planted a seed,
In spring it will grow.
Now it's asleep
Under the

Use each set of rhyming words in a poem.

Day at the Beach

sand _____

hand _____

run _____

fun _____

Flying a Kite

kite _____

right _____

play _____

day _____

0-7424-1802-2 *Building Grammar & Writing Skills*

Answer Key

Bountiful Blends (Page 9)
1. blue, crayon   2. swing, tree
3. play, snow   4. snail, crawl
5. skunk, flower

Treasure Teams (Page 10)
1. ship, shoe, fish   2. chick, chair, chime
3. thumb, tooth, bath   4. graph, photo, phone

Vowel Venture (Page 11)
1. ape   2. elephant   3. insect
4. owl   5. umbrella   Students' words will vary.

Short Vowels (Page 12)
1. sand   2. bucket   3. fish
4. clam   5. shell   6. castle
7. umbrella   8. crab

Zoo Clues (Page 13)

Sneaky, Silent E (Page 14)
1. Staci <u>ate</u> the crunchy apple.
2. The clown gave Tom a candy <u>cane</u>.
3. I want to fly my <u>kite</u>.
4. Jared took <u>care</u> of his puppy.
5. <u>Ripe</u> peaches are good to eat.
6. Mom wrote a <u>note</u> to my teacher.
7. The <u>pine</u> tree is green.
8. Sara's new kitten is so <u>cute</u>!

Letter Practice (Page 15)
Red: R B A S N T U I X F Y Z H L Q D E V M W
G P K O
Blue: d k v b y l r i a q c e f g h j m n o p w x

Starting Sentences (Page 16)
1. Birds fly south in winter.
2. My grandfather is funny.
3. Yesterday it rained.
4. The girl ate a sandwich.
5. River rafting is fun for the whole family.
6. Andy's dog won a blue ribbon.
7. Summer is my favorite season.
8. High wind blew down the sign.
9. Do you like popcorn?
10. Run really fast!

Capital "I" (Page 17)
Kaitlyn wanted to make pancakes for breakfast
with her dad. They took out the <u>ingredients</u>. They
were out of <u>milk</u>. "<u>I</u> will drive to the store," her
dad said. <u>While</u> he was gone, <u>Kaitlyn</u> measured
the other <u>ingredients</u>. "<u>I</u> am back, "her dad <u>said</u>.
"<u>I</u> am glad you are," <u>Kaitlyn</u> replied. "<u>I</u> am getting
very hungry. May <u>I</u> pour the <u>milk</u>?" Dad handed
her the <u>milk</u>. She <u>mixed</u> the batter and poured <u>it</u>
on the <u>griddle</u>. Dad <u>flipped</u> pancakes as they
cooked. They ate the pancakes <u>with</u> maple syrup.
"These are the best pancakes <u>I</u> have ever tasted,"
Dad <u>said</u>. "<u>I think</u> you are <u>right</u>," <u>Kaitlyn</u> agreed
with a <u>smile</u>.

Names and Places (Page 18)
1. Dear <u>Paul</u>,
We are having lots of fun in <u>Montana</u>. We went
fishing at the <u>Choro River</u>. We saw the <u>Sawtooth</u>
<u>Mountains</u>. Tonight we are going to stay in

<u>Helena</u>. That is the state capital.
Your friend,
<u>Angela</u>

<u>Paul Davis</u>
<u>555 Porter Street</u>
<u>Davis</u>, <u>Delaware</u> 12345

2. Dear <u>Mom</u> and <u>Dad</u>,
I love <u>Camp Azalea</u>! We went for a hike in <u>Red</u>
<u>Rock Valley</u>. Tomorrow I want to visit the <u>Dean</u>
<u>Thomas Library</u>. It has lots of books about dogs. I
miss <u>Buddy</u>. Give him a pat on the head for me.
Love,
<u>Dylan</u>

<u>Mr.</u> and <u>Mrs. Worski</u>
<u>123 Covington Court</u>
<u>Mayfield</u>, <u>Texas</u> 54321

Tricky Titles (Page 19)
Doctor Waldo Brown Mrs. Anita Alonzo
Mr. George Lipton   Cousin Sara
Uncle Frederick   Aunt Tanya
Ms. Tarkington   Professor Elder
Miss Julia Ames   Dr. Amelia Wentworth

Books and Magazines (Page 20)
1. How Much Is That Doggie in the Window?
2. The Biography of Helen Keller
3. Horse Lover Magazine
4. Green Eggs and Ham
5. Twinkle, Twinkle Little Star
6. The Big Book of Lizards
7. Mary Had a Little Lamb
8. How to Train Your Cat with Treats
9. School Days Magazine
10. America the Beautiful

Calendar Capitals (Page 21)
1. <u>Allen</u> goes to soccer practice on <u>Tuesdays</u> and
<u>Thursdays</u>. 2. <u>We</u> celebrate <u>Fourth</u> of <u>July</u> by
boating on the lake. 3. <u>Jenn's</u> dance recital is on
<u>Valentine's Day</u>. 4. <u>Kelly</u> went to <u>Ellen's</u> house on
<u>Friday</u>. 5. <u>My</u> sister will be six years old in <u>May</u>.
6. In <u>January</u>, we always go sledding <u>Saturday</u>
mornings. 7. <u>Jamie's</u> favorite holiday is
<u>Hanukah</u>, which comes in <u>December</u>. 8.–10.
Sentences will vary.

Ready for Review (Page 22)
1. <u>My</u> friends and I go to <u>Bear Creek School</u>.
2. <u>Byron</u> has a dog named <u>Tilly</u> and a cat named
<u>Weed</u>. 3. <u>My</u> teacher is <u>Mrs. Jamison</u>. 4. <u>Jerry</u>
went to <u>Wyoming</u> last year for <u>Father's Day</u>.
5. <u>Alicia</u> read <u>The Wind in the Willows</u>. 6. <u>Aunt</u>
<u>Cindy</u> is my favorite aunt. 7. <u>Brandon</u> celebrates
<u>Christmas</u> with his grandparents. 8. <u>Tina</u> wrote a
poem called <u>Jumpy Bumpy Jack</u>. 9. <u>Dr. Lopez</u>
made a special visit to see <u>Rex</u> last <u>Saturday</u>.
10. <u>Mother's Day</u> is in the month of <u>May</u>.

At the End (Page 23)
1. Hawaii is the fiftieth state.
2. Sit down.
4. William read his book quietly.
6. Do your homework neatly.
7. My dog has floppy ears.
8. Read your book.
9. My dad snores.

Long to Short (Page 24)

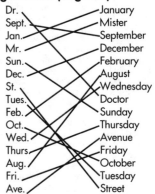

Dr.   January
Sept.   Mister
Jan.   September
Mr.   December
Sun.   February
Dec.   August
St.   Wednesday
Tues.   Doctor
Feb.   Sunday
Oct.   Thursday
Wed.   Avenue
Thurs.   Friday
Aug.   October
Fri.   Tuesday
Ave.   Street

What's the Question? (Page 25)
2. Did you eat lunch yet?
4. Are you cold?
5. How old is Jonathan's sister?
6. Where does Natalie live?
8. Why did Frank write in his book?
10. Where is my pen?
Sentences will vary.

Exciting Exclamations (Page 26)
1. I can't believe we won! 2. I don't like this
book. 3. That is nice. 4. Do you want to keep
it? 5. Wow, it's just what I wanted! 6. It's so
cold! 7. I don't like that book. 8. Watch out!
9. Is that your glass? 10. May I help you? 11.
I can't believe we won! 12. Wow, it's just what I
wanted! 13. Watch out! 14. It's so cold!

Sentence Endings (Page 27)
1. That bunny is so cute! 2. Do you have a pet?
3. My cat loves tuna fish. 4. I think turtles are
fun. 5. Look at that! 6. Have you ever seen a
ferret? 7. How much does that birdcage cost?
8. My dog likes to ride in the car. 9. Wow, his
teeth are sharp! 10. I know the owner of this pet
store. 11.–13. Sentences will vary.

Pause for Commas (Page 28)
It's a birthday party!
Cassie Wyman
Date: October 9, 2002
423 Center Street
Place: Pizza Paradise
Littleton, Maine 89764

You're invited to a sleepover!
Lin Nance
Date: January 23, 2003
37 West Road
Place: My house
Tampa, Florida 62341

Boo! It's a Halloween party!
Tyrone Hilliard
Date: October 31, 2003
10024 Wells Avenue
Place: My house
Claremont, California 91734

Splish, splash! Come to my pool party!
Armando Santos
Date: June 16, 2003
562 Justice Street, #38
Place: Manfield Park
West Orange, NJ 07052

125

0-7424-1802-2 *Building Grammar & Writing Skills*

Answer Key

Make a List (Page 29)
1. My mother grows roses, daisies, and violets in her garden. 2. My brother's name is John Henry Mills. 3. There are maple, pine, oak, and elm trees on my street. 4. In my class we study spelling, math, history, and art. 5. Claire, Phil, Tammy, Joe, and I went to the movies together. 6. Tana brought her dogs Peaches, Romeo, and Clyde to the park. 7. Mina's favorite colors are yellow, purple, blue, and pink. 8.–10. Sentences will vary.

Whose Is It? (Page 30)
Cameron and Marie were playing in the park near a tree. The tree's leaves were thick and green. Cameron saw a bird's nest in the tree. Marie saw a squirrel in the tree. The squirrel's fur was soft and gray. A small dog ran across the grass toward them. The dog's leash dragged on the ground. The dog's owner ran behind. "Sorry!" he called when he caught the leash. "I guess everyone loves the park," Marie laughed.

Quote Me (Page 31)
1. "Jill won a medal," yelled the coach.
2. Todd said, "I like dogs."
3. "I'm going to walk to school," said Sue.
4. "Hit the ball!" Bryan yelled at his little brother.
5. "I love apple pie," Emma told me.

Ready for Review (Page 32)
Mando put paper(,) a pencil(,) an eraser(,) and markers on his desk(.) (He) was going to start his report on President Abraham (L)incoln(.) He wrote the date February 16(,) 1809. (")That is when Lincoln was born,(") he said aloud to his cat, Simba(.) (")(W)ould you like to know more about him(?) You'll just have to wait until I finish my report." Mando reached down to scratch (S)imba on the neck, and the cat purred and purred. (")Okay, back to work," (M)ando said.

Pretty Presents (Page 33)

Person, Place, or Thing? (Page 34)
1. A frog lives in the pond.
2. My teacher drives a truck.
3. The girl ate a hot dog.
4. The doctor walked me to my car.
5. The street is lined with trees.
6. That box is full of trash.
7. The ocean is full of colorful fish.
8. The player threw the football down the field.

Person: teacher, girl, doctor, player
Place: pond, ocean, street, field
Thing: frog, truck, hot dog, car, trees, box, trash, fish, football

Practice with Nouns (Page 35)
1. The boy plays soccer. 2. I planted a vegetable garden. 3. My sister planted a tree at school. 4. These gloves are red and white. 5. My grandma gave us cookies and milk after lunch. 6. My aunt visited the museum last fall. 7. Please wear a sweater. 8. Sometimes I read a book in bed. 9. She bought milk, eggs, bread, and fruit at the store. 10. That dog chased my kite all over the park. 11. pig 12. sun 13. flower 14. bee 15. drum 16. bed

Common or Proper? (Page 36)
1. April P   2. dog C
3. Wednesday P 4. Fifi P
5. Pacific P   6. lake P
7. boy C   8. Italy P
9. Randi P   10. flower C
11. country C   12. Smokey P
13. New York P 14. May P
15. state C

Proper Places (Page 37)
1. New York City
2. Orange County
3. Lake Superior; United States
4. Chloe; Camp Willow
5. Ted; Chicago; Sears Tower
6. Bermuda; Atlantic Ocean
7. Michigan; Lansing
8. Lewis Park
9. Ellis Elementary School
10. Chelsea; Colorado River

Days and Dates (Page 38)
Days: Monday, Friday, Sunday, Thursday, Tuesday, Wednesday
Months: June, April, December, February, January
Holidays: Mother's Day, President's Day, Labor Day, Valentine's Day, Halloween

Towers of Nouns (Page 39)
1. Laurie, Park Ave., Ford, Ohio
2. 3rd Street, Mrs. Poole, Monday, Yolanda
3. Coach Gorman, Disneyland, Indian Ocean, Tuesday, Fluffy
4. Buddy, Oregon, Times Square, Crater Lake
5.–8. Sentences will vary.

How Many? (Page 40)
1. three flowers 2. two clocks 3. six bats
4. four pencils 5. two books 6. three snakes
7. five hats 8. four balls 9. two birds
10. three apples

More Than One (Page 41)
1. kiss; kisses   2. watch; watches
3. bus; buses   4. fox; foxes
5. wash; washes   6. grass; grasses
7. bush; bushes   8. box; boxes

Plenty of Plurals (Page 42)
1. dolls   2. boxes
3. dresses   4. waves
5. brushes   6. wishes
7. buses   8. parks
9. dishes   10. shoes

Special Plurals (Page 43)
1. monkeys   2. parties
3. babies   4. turkeys
5. valleys   6. stories
7. flies   8. cries

Ready for Review (Page 44)

			C			T		
			A			U		
	F		T			R		
C	L	A	S	S	E	S		
I	M					K		
T	R	I	P	S		E		
I	I			T		Y		
E	I		F	A	X	E	S	
S	E			G				
S	P	E	E	C	H	E	S	
	S							

Verbs in Action (Page 45)
1. I hop over the fence.
2. Jack climbs the ladder.
3. Do not play in the hallway.
4. Jamie can run very fast.
5. Natalie works on her painting.
6. Terrell loves potato chips.
7. We shop on Sundays.
8. Lindsey draws very well.

C	T	L	O	R	U	N	J	N	S
L	O	V	E	S	D	C	E	H	H
I	S	T	P	V	R	N	R	E	O
M	J	P	L	L	A	H	H	I	P
B	Q	N	A	V	W	O	R	K	S
S	W	G	Y	Y	S	P	R	O	W

More Verbs (Page 46)
1. Sometimes I dream while I am asleep.
2. I do not believe in space aliens.
3. I live in a house near my school.
4. The teacher asked us to listen to the music.
5. Did you hear that loud noise?
6. What do you think about this book?
7. I would like to learn to play the piano.
8. I know how to say the Pledge of Allegiance.
9. Will you help me plan my birthday party?
10. I want to go to the movies today.

Now and Then (Page 47)
helped   washed   moved   barked
cleaned   loved   jumped   waited
missed   danced   smiled   hoped
Sentences will vary.

In the Past (Page 48)
1. hugged 2. stepped 3. stopped 4. batted
5. popped 6. flapped 7. skated 8. dusted
9. petted

A Little Help (Page 49)
1. Next week I (will) sing in the school talent show. 2. Someday I (will) teach my dog to fetch. 3. After school Carter (can) come to my house to play. 4. (Can) you watch the movie with me tonight? 5. Amy (will) write her report after class. 6. The bird (can) fly now that its wing is healed. 7. The sun (will) rise tomorrow. 8. In January we (can) go to the mountains. 9. Patrick (can) run in the next race. 10. I (will) eat pizza for dinner.

Is, Am, Are (Page 50)
1. Jenna is a great dancer. 2. We are going on vacation. 3. My grandparents are moving next door. 4. I am tired today. 5. The cat is sleeping in the sun. 6. The flower is yellow. 7. I am happy. 8. Those puppies are playful.

Was and Were (Page 51)
Last week Paul, Dina, and I went to the beach. We were so excited! The day was sunny and warm. I was collecting seashells when a huge wave crashed on the shore. Dina and I were soaked! The water was very cold. Paul was laughing. Another wave crashed ashore, and he was soaked, too! Then we were all laughing. After that, Dina and Paul were hungry, so we stopped to eat lunch. I was late getting home, but it was worth it. It was a great day!

Has, Have, Had (Page 52)
1. N   2. N   3. P   4. N
5. N   6. P   7. P   8. N
9. P   10. N

0-7424-1802-2 *Building Grammar & Writing Skills*

Answer Key

Match It! (Page 53)
1. Izzy <u>drinks</u> milk with her dinner.
2. Angela <u>bakes</u> cookies with her mother.
3. Dad <u>drives</u> me to school.
4. Eddie and his brother <u>share</u> a bedroom.
5. Our team <u>wears</u> red uniforms.
6. My grandparents <u>live</u> next door.
7. The house <u>looks</u> old.
8. Can you <u>play</u> the piano?
9. I <u>wash</u> my hands before I eat.
10. Jeff <u>sits</u> in the front row.

Ready for Review (Page 54)
Purple: bike, closet, crayon, dog, water, shirt, sister, nose, friend
Yellow: sleep, push, think, drive, sit, write, draw, ride, is

Pronoun Power (Page 55)
1. <u>He</u> found his mittens.
2. <u>She</u> loves <u>them</u>.
3. Then <u>they</u> went back inside.
4. <u>She</u> laughed at <u>it</u>.
5. <u>She</u> went with <u>him</u> many times.
6. The team cheered for <u>us</u>.
7. <u>They</u> walked for an hour.
8. <u>They</u> named <u>him</u> Leroy.

All About Me (Page 56)
1. (I gave) a birthday present <u>to Wendy</u>.
2. (Wendy gave) her pencil <u>to me</u>.
3. (Marcia and I bought) ice-cream cones.
4. (Jan went) <u>with Marcia and me</u>.
5. (Justin took) a picture <u>of me</u>.
6. (I took) a picture <u>of the mountains</u>.
7. Colin and I helped with the dishes.
8. Mom made Gretchen and <u>me</u> a sandwich.
9. I like Laura.
10. Laura likes <u>me</u>.
11. Dad helped <u>me</u> with my homework.
12. <u>I</u> like to do homework.

It's All Mine (Page 57)
Mrs. Wyatt's second grade class had a science fair. Dylan made a volcano. <u>His</u> (volcano) had pretend lava. Sheri and Sue showed how to make sugar crystals. <u>Their</u> (project) was small. Lee grew a plant. He painted some of the leaves. "<u>Your</u> (projects) are all very good," Mrs. Wyatt said. "But <u>their</u> (tags) are all mixed up." "The (plant) is <u>mine</u>," said Lee. "I know the (volcano) is <u>yours</u>," Mrs. Wyatt told Dylan. "Which (project) is <u>yours</u>?" she asked Sheri.

"The crystal (garden) is <u>ours</u>," replied Sheri and Sue.

Describing Words (Page 58)
Answers will vary.

Two Big, Round Blue Eyes (Page 59)
Size: small, tall, big, wide, tiny
Shape: square, round, flat, squiggly, oval
Color: pink, yellow, white, green, silver
Number: three, five, two, one, six

All These Adjectives (Page 60)
1. The stories were <u>scary</u>.
2. I am <u>hungry</u>.
3. The thunder was <u>loud</u>.
4. The trees were <u>green</u>.
5. The elephant is <u>fat</u>.
6. The children are <u>excited</u>.
7. Jessie was <u>happy</u> on her birthday.
8. The weather was <u>cold</u> yesterday. OR Yesterday the weather was <u>cold</u>.
9. The light was <u>bright</u>.
10. I am <u>tired</u>.

Comparing with Adjectives (Page 61)
1. Eddie is <u>younger</u> than Joe.
2. The library is the <u>tallest</u> building in town.
3. Lakota is <u>faster</u> than Midnight.
4. Ralph's flashlight is the <u>brightest</u>.
5. Andra's hair is <u>longer</u> than Madison's.
6. Jordan can throw <u>harder</u> than me.
7. Sam and Linita are the <u>smartest</u> in the class.
8. Our classroom is <u>colder</u> than theirs.
9. Patti is the <u>greatest</u> athlete in the school.
10. The cake is <u>sweeter</u> than the pie.

All About Adverbs (Page 62)
Answers will vary.

Ready for Review (Page 63)
1. Our <u>slow</u> mail carrier delivered our mail (late).
2. I ate the <u>hot</u> soup (slowly).
3. The <u>sneaky</u> snake slithered (quietly) through the forest.
4. Angela (often) wrote <u>long</u> letters.
5. Darryl curled up (under) the <u>warm blue</u> blanket.
6. The <u>new</u> supermarket opens (early).
7. <u>Fluffy white</u> snow drifted (lazily).
8. (Yesterday) Denny baked a <u>chocolate</u> cake.
9. My <u>older</u> cousin Anna will be here (soon).
10. Rebecca placed her <u>pink</u> umbrella (behind) the <u>big</u> door.
11. We ran (quickly) to the <u>big</u> museum (before) it closed.
12. She (always) writes the <u>best</u> papers in the class.

A, An, The (Page 64)
1. a fish 2. a wish 3. a mask
4. an oven 5. an umbrella 6. a wolf
7. a planet 8. an arm 9. an oar
10. a tooth 11. I went to <u>a</u> movie.
12. The hen laid <u>an</u> egg.
13. When <u>the</u> alarm clock rings, I get up.
14. My mom went to this school <u>a</u> long time ago.
15. This is <u>the</u> movie I want you to see.

Multiple Meanings (Page 65)
1. noun; adverb 2. noun; noun
3. noun; verb 4. verb; noun
5. noun; verb 6. adjective; verb
7. noun; verb 8. noun; adverb

Crazy Compounds (Page 66)
1. bathroom, bedroom, bluebird, birdbath
2. sunrise, flashlight, lighthouse, doghouse, sunlight
3. sandbox, boxcar, shoebag, shoebox
4. pancake, cupcake, teapot, teacup, flowerpot
5. doorway, doorknob, doorbell, hallway

Silly Synonyms (Page 67)
1. sloppy 2. hot 3. bug 4. sad
5. tree 6. gray 7. whisper 8. cry

Observing Opposites (Page 68)

Sounds the Same (Page 69)
1. Would you like to <u>meet</u> my friend?
2. Gail wore a <u>blue</u> dress.
3. My brother is <u>four</u> years old.
4. The <u>sun</u> helps plants make food.
5. <u>Would</u> you like some ice cream?
6. We <u>ate</u> pizza for lunch.
7. I have a <u>new</u> pair of shoes.
8. I don't <u>know</u> the answer.
9. It isn't polite to <u>stare</u>.
10. Can you tie a square <u>knot</u>?
11. I have to <u>write</u> a letter to my grandfather.
12. Wesley <u>rode</u> his bicycle to school.

There, Their, They're (Page 70)
1. there 2. Their 3. They're 4. their
5. They're 6. there 7. there 8. they're
9. their 10. Their

Your and You're (Page 71)
1. You're 2. your 3. You're 4. Your
5. your 6. You're 7. your 8. you're
9. your 10. your

Two, To, Too (Page 72)
1. Gabriel is going <u>to</u> catch the ball.
4. Monkeys love <u>to</u> eat bananas.

Rhyme Time (Page 73)
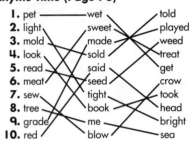

1. pet — wet
2. light
3. mold
4. look
5. read
6. meat
7. sew
8. tree
9. grade
10. red

(sweet, made, sold, said, seed, tight, book, me, blow)
(told, played, weed, treat, get, crow, took, head, bright, sea)

Writing Rhymes (Page 74)
1. To make a cake, You have to <u>bake</u>.
2. In Grandma's <u>house</u> There is a <u>mouse</u>.
3. When I sleep at night, I turn off the <u>light</u>.
4. My Aunt Lou Works at the <u>zoo</u>.
5. To clean my room, I'll need a <u>broom</u>.
6. I'll sit down there In that green <u>chair</u>.

Blooming Words (Page 75)
she'll—she will
aren't—are not
it's—it is
he's—he is
wasn't—was not
we're—we are
you're—you are
she's—she is
isn't—is not
I'm—I am

Creating Contractions (Page 76)
1. We <u>can't</u> use the park bench until the paint is dry. 2. Becky <u>isn't</u> feeling well. 3. <u>Don't</u> run near the pool. 4. Paula and her brother <u>weren't</u> at the football game. 5. <u>I'm</u> seven years old. 6. <u>You'll</u> love this new game. 7. Bishop said <u>he's</u> happy to go back to school. 8. Brenda wants to know if <u>you've</u> finished music class. 9. <u>It's</u> snowing! 10. Dinner <u>won't</u> be ready until later.

In the Index (Page 99)
1. pages 5, 19, 29, 35, 39 2. yes 3. jaguars (one possible answer) 4. yes 5. no 6. yes 7. page 31 8. three-toed sloth, capuchin monkey, birds 9. page 47 10. yes

Simple Subjects (Page 77)
1. <u>The trees on Ames Street</u> are very tall.
2. <u>Jessie and Arlo</u> had hamburgers for lunch.
3. <u>The old town library</u> is being painted.
4. <u>A tall woman</u> was carrying a flag.
5. <u>A large dust cloud</u> rose in the air.
6. <u>Brie</u> laughed until she cried.
7.–12. Answers will vary.

Awesome Action (Page 78)
1. The big green crocodile <u>gobbled up</u> a fish.
2. Ms. Angelo's class <u>planted</u> a garden.
3. The boy <u>carved</u> the huge pumpkin.
4. The baker <u>rolled out</u> the dough.
5. Stephen <u>spilled</u> milk on his new sweater.
6. The gray whale <u>flipped</u> its tail in the water.
7.–12. Answers will vary.

0-7424-1802-2 Building Grammar & Writing Skills

Answer Key

Complete Sentences (Page 79)
1. Mrs. Bell's dog begs on its hind legs!
2. A flock of birds flew over the park.
3. My grandfather can play the violin.
4. The cowboy wore fancy boots.
5. When I was five, I visited Australia.
6. The man in the black shirt ran for the bus.

Incomplete Sentences (Page 80)
Gabe wanted to get home early. His Uncle Ted was coming to visit. <u>Used to live in Montana.</u> Uncle Ted told great stories. Gabe ran faster. <u>When he raced up the steps.</u> There was Uncle Ted. He was eating a sandwich. "Hi, Uncle Ted," Gabe said happily. "Hi Gabe," his uncle answered. <u>Been waiting for you.</u> We are going to go camping. "Hooray!" Gabe cried. "I'll get my sleeping bag." They packed food and warm clothes. <u>Packed plenty of it.</u> They drove to the campsite. <u>A river nearby.</u> They set up the tent and built a fire. Uncle Ted told stories about Montana. <u>About a big black bear.</u> When Gabe was sleepy, he curled up in his sleeping bag. As he fell asleep he thought he heard a bear. <u>In the morning.</u> "I dreamed about a bear," Gabe told his uncle. "Your dream left footprints," said Uncle Ted. <u>Near the tent.</u> "Wow," Gabe said with a smile. "Now I'll have a story to tell."

It's Telling (Page 81)
1. <u>Amber</u> woke up early.
2. It was snowing.
3. <u>She</u> dressed in warm clothes.
4. <u>Lin</u> and <u>Tyrone</u> built a snowman.
5. <u>Karen</u> loves hot chocolate.
6. <u>The black dog</u> played in the snow.
7. <u>Allie</u> made snow angels.
8. <u>The pond</u> is frozen.
9. <u>Haley</u> is a good ice skater.
10. <u>Alex</u> lost her fuzzy green mittens.
Sentences will vary.

Asking Questions (Page 82)
1. <u>Who</u> missed the bus?
2. <u>Why/Who/How/What</u> did Elisa leave?
3. <u>How old</u> are you?
4. <u>Why/When/How</u> is Mia wearing your sweater?
5. <u>Who/What</u> is in that box?
6. <u>Why/How/Where/When</u> did you do that?
7. <u>What</u> did Garret say?
8. <u>When/How/Why/Where</u> did you hurt your arm?
Sentences will vary.

Change It Around (Page 83)
1. The kitten is sitting on the chair.
2. The fish is in the water.
3. The boy threw the baseball.
4. Greta spread jam on bread.
5. Candace found toy bears on her bed.
6. The crowd yelled as the player ran around the bases.

Ready for Review (Page 84)
1. Soledad painted a picture of her cat. **T**
2. Do you like strawberries? **A**
3. Scott plays piano well. **T**
4. ~~Under the tree near the river~~
5. What is your address? **A**
6. March is a windy month. **T**
7. What time is it? **A**
8. ~~The girl with the brown hair~~
9. Are you sure? **A**
10. Stephanie has a rock collection. **T**

Combining Sentences (Page 85)
1. Juan found a cricket and a ladybug in his backyard. **2.** Britney likes math <u>and</u> art. **3.** We might have pizza <u>or</u> salad for lunch. **4.** I ran to school, <u>but</u> I was late. **5.** Dennis <u>and</u> Tony went to Ann's birthday party. **6.** I saw you, <u>but</u> I didn't hear what you said.

The Main Idea (Page 86)
1. Jessica spilled the milk.
2. Grandpa helped the boy fish.
3. Greta and Tim painted Buddy's doghouse.
4. Sally Squirrel paints acorns.

Important Ideas (Page 87)
1. He doesn't have any friends.
2. Maggie wants to surprise her dad for his birthday.
3. Today is the day he will get his fish tank.

Reading a Recipe (Page 88)
10—Let muffins cool.
3—Then add eggs, milk, and oil.
9—Take muffin pan out of oven.
4—Put fresh blueberries in last.
2—Put flour and sugar in bowl.
6—Pour batter in muffin pan.
1—Get out ingredients.
7—Put muffin pan in oven.
8—Bake for 30 minutes.
5—Stir batter until it is all mixed together.

Story Order (Page 89)
3—Ian walked Sparky down the street and to the park.
7—Sparky splashed into the water.
10—"I know what we are doing next," Ian said. "You need a bath."
4—They walked to the pond at the center of the park.
2—Ian clipped Sparky's new red leash on her collar.
9—Sparky pranced out of the pond covered in mud.
6—She barked and pulled at her leash until it slipped from Ian's hand.
5—Sparky saw a flock of wild ducks in the water.
1—Ian decided to go for a walk with his dog, Sparky.
8—The ducks quacked, flapped, and flew away.

Organize the Animals (Page 90)
Wild Animals: tiger, elephant, giraffe, hippo
Farm Animals: cow, chicken, pig, sheep
Pets: dog, cat, canary, hamster

What Doesn't Belong? (Page 91)

Perfect Paragraph (Page 92)
Circle sentences 1, 3, 5, 6, 8, 9.

Tricky Topics (Page 93)
1. My grandfather knows a lot about horses.
2. Yesterday I had a tough day.

In the End (Page 94)
1. Today would be a good day to fly our kites.
2. Ending sentences will vary.

Beginning, Middle, and End (Page 95)
Answers will vary.

Finding Facts (Page 96)
1. Y	2. N	3. Y	4. Y
5. N	6. Y	7. Y	8. N
9. Y	10. N		

Clever Clues (Page 97)
Corey—Pioneers
Taylor—Rain Forest
Mateo—Space
Marcus—Mexico
Rosa—Oceans
Ray—Mountains

Table of Contents (Page 98)
1. pages 36–39 **2.** pages 44–46 **3.** pages 16–21
4. no **5.** lightning **6.** pages 3–4
7. glossary **8.** pages 12–15 **9.** climate
10. 48 pages

Using a Dictionary (Page 100)
1. bib, cat, dish, fish
2. house, ice, jump, kettle
3. map, mop, nap, oar
4. pair, peach, pour, pumpkin
5. apple, bunch, coal, egg
6. umbrella, yellow, zebra, zoo
7. vase, vote, whale, whistle
8. face, fall, grape, icicle

Guiding Words (Page 101)
mare, margin, marine, mark, market, marsh, mascot, mash, mask, mass
Cross out the words *make* and *mat.*

Organize an Outline (Page 102)
Answers can be listed in any order under the correct topics.
1. Winter
   A. icicles
   B. snowman
   C. January
2. Spring
   A. chicks
   B. flowers
   C. May
3. Summer
   A. July
   B. swimming
   C. ice cream
4. Fall
   A. Thanksgiving
   B. falling leaves
   C. November

Writing a Report (Page 103)
1. library **2.** encyclopedia
3. magazine **4.** book
5. internet **6.** teacher
7. scientist **8.** museum
9. television
10. savanna or grassland; woodlands; taiga or woodlands
11. meat; grasses; grasses and leaves

Dear Friend (Page 104)
Letters will vary.

The Story of Me (Page 105)
Stories will vary.

In My Journal (Page 106)
Journal entries will vary.

Write It Right (Page 107)
Lorenzo couldn(')t wait to go to the book fair at his school. (E)very year there was a guessing jar(.) Lorenzo was sure that he could guess the right number. "(T)he prize is a basket of books,(") he told his friend (B)ryan. "I know (I) will win. All I have to do is guess. Are you going to enter(?)" "(I')ll try," Bryan said. (A)fter school Lorenzo went to the fair. (H)e found the guessing jar and tried to count all the marbles inside. He wrote a guess on (an) entry slip. He crossed his (fingers) and dropped the slip into the entry box. The next day (L)orenzo received a telephone call(.) (")(I)t is for you," his mom said with a smile. Lorenzo listened to the caller(,) and then he smiled (too). "I won(!)" he shouted. (")Now all I have to do is read all (those) books."

Pages 108–113
Answers will vary.

Tell a Story (Page 114)
1. Tatiana
2. Jeremy
3. Tatiana's home
4. No one came to her party.
5. She forgot to send the invitations.

Pages 115–124
Answers will vary.

0-7424-1802-2 *Building Grammar & Writing Skills*